Anonymous

Exhibition of Pictures by Masters of the Flemish and British Schools

Including a Selection from the Works of Sir Peter Paul Rubens

Anonymous

Exhibition of Pictures by Masters of the Flemish and British Schools
Including a Selection from the Works of Sir Peter Paul Rubens

ISBN/EAN: 9783337226350

Printed in Europe, USA, Canada, Australia, Japan

Cover: Foto ©Thomas Meinert / pixelio.de

More available books at **www.hansebooks.com**

Exhibition of Pictures

BY MASTERS OF THE

Flemish and British Schools

INCLUDING

A SELECTION FROM THE WORKS

OF

SIR PETER PAUL RUBENS

THE NEW GALLERY

REGENT STREET

1899—1900

RICHARD CLAY AND SONS, LIMITED,
LONDON AND BUNGAY.

THE NEW GALLERY

Arrangement of the Exhibition.

WEST ROOM.
PICTURES OF THE EARLY FLEMISH SCHOOL, AND ANTIQUE AND
MEDIAEVAL OBJECTS OF ART.

NORTH ROOM.
PICTURES AND DRAWINGS BY SIR PETER PAUL RUBENS, ETC.

SOUTH ROOM.
PICTURES OF THE BRITISH SCHOOL.

CENTRAL HALL.
EMBROIDERY AND NEEDLEWORK.

BALCONY.
PICTURES OF THE EARLY FLEMISH SCHOOL.

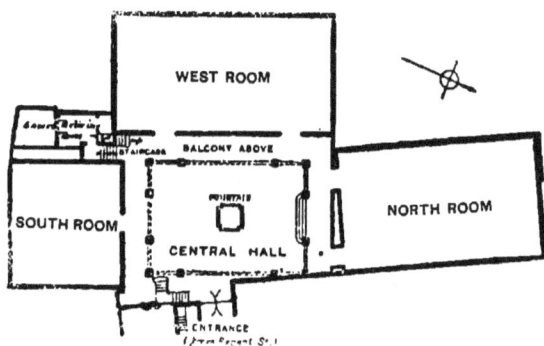

PREFATORY NOTE.

The third centenary of the birth of Anthony Van Dyck having fallen in the year 1899, the event was celebrated at Antwerp by a general exhibition of that artist's works, and a similar collection has been formed by the Royal Academy for exhibition this winter at Burlington House. The Directors of the New Gallery consider this an opportune occasion to complete the representation of the Flemish School by bringing together examples of the Early or Gothic School, and also of Van Dyck's illustrious predecessor and master, Peter Paul Rubens.

As a supplement to the exhibitions of the two great artists, Rubens and Van Dyck, to whom the art of portrait and landscape painting in this country owes so much, a small collection has been formed of pictures of the British School.

The Directors and Secretary of the New Gallery wish to tender their most grateful thanks to the owners of pictures here and in Belgium, who have so kindly assisted them in carrying out their scheme and enabled them to offer so many choice works in illustration of the schools they have desired to represent this winter. They also wish to convey their thanks to Mr. W. H. Weale for his introductory notes on the Flemish School of Painting, and to him and Sir Charles Robinson and Mr. Herbert Cook for the assistance they have given in forming the Collection.

As on previous occasions, the historical notes and descriptions of the pictures in the Catalogue are compiled by Mr. Herbert Grueber, to whom the Directors again wish to convey their most sincere thanks.

Whilst the Exhibition was in course of arrangement the sad news of the death of the Duke of Westminster was announced. The Directors wish to record the deep sense of sorrow they feel at the loss of one who not only invariably placed his valuable collection of pictures at their disposal, but was also a kind friend to the New Gallery in many other ways.

LEONARD C. LINDSAY,
Secretary.

EARLY ART IN THE NETHERLANDS

ART in the Low Countries—that is, in the present kingdoms of the Netherlands and Belgium and the adjacent districts of France which formerly formed part of the counties of Flanders and Hainault—was in the seventh and eighth centuries practised with success in several great monasteries, such as those at Coeln, Echternach, Stavelot, Fosses, Lobbes, Tournay and Ghent, all of which were real centres of civilization and culture. Two manuscript Gospel books on vellum, of the seventh century, adorned with illuminations and miniatures which show a considerable amount of skill, are preserved in the church of Maaseyck. They were executed by two sainted sisters, Harlindis and Relindis, abbesses of Aldeneyck. It was, however, Charles the Great who gave the first great impulse to art. He gathered about him artists from Constantinople, Italy and England, to adorn his palaces at Nijmwegen and at Aachen, established a school of art which was attached to his court, and in 8ɔ7 not only issued a decree that all churches should be adorned with paintings, but appointed inspectors to see that his orders were carried out. Monastic chronicles of the tenth, eleventh and twelfth centuries record the execution of many mural paintings; one of these, representing a miracle of Saint Martin of Tours, was still to be seen in the seventeenth century in the church bearing his name at Liége. The emperors Otho II. and Otho III. (972-1002) employed at their court several Byzantine artists; one of these named John adorned the Carlovingian church at Aachen and the choir of the abbey of S. James at Liége with mural paintings. All these have disappeared, but a strong Byzantine influence is evident in many works of art which have escaped destruction; some of these, such as the ivory panels at Liége and Tongres, and the rock-crystal intaglio of King Lothair, now in the British Museum, may not have been executed in the Low Countries, but others, as, for instance, the enamelled plaques on the shrine of Saint Mark at Huy, the ivory diptych of Genoels Elderen now in the Museum at Brussels, and the Gospels of Stavelot in the Royal Library at Brussels, were certainly executed in the country. A large number of other illuminated manuscripts enable us to trace the gradual development of local pictorial art; one good example, a Bible in two large folio volumes, written, illuminated, adorned with miniatures, and bound by two monks of the abbey of Stavelot, Goderan and Ernest, occupied their working hours during four years and was completed in 1097. It is now in the British Museum (Add. MSS. 28106 and 28107). Numerous other illuminated manuscripts executed in the monasteries of the Netherlands are still preserved in public and private libraries and in the churches of Belgium. Many more have been destroyed since the middle of the sixteenth century.

Up to the end of the twelfth century Art in the Low Countries was almost entirely[1] under the control of the monastic orders. The abbeys, and even many of the priories, had around them a large number of dependents who worked for and under the direction of the monks, who always had two schools; one in which they trained their own novices in the Arts and Sciences, the other in which they instructed their dependents in every craft. There is documentary evidence to show that these dependents living under the protection of the abbot were to be counted by hundreds, and sometimes even by thousands. They formed communities working, not only for the monks, but also, under strict regulations, for outsiders. Towards the end of the twelfth century a great change took place—a change brought about by the development of the towns. As soon as a town grew to any size the inhabitants engaged in any particular craft, or in two or more connected crafts, joined themselves into associations to protect their common interests. These associations, once formed, gradually developed, and when the commonalty obtained from the sovereign a charter of incorporation, they, in their turn, got one from the municipality. The first thing a newly-incorporated municipality did was to build a belfry and then a town hall; other public buildings soon had to be added; and as the inhabitants grew in wealth they replaced their

[1] At Maastricht, Liége, Utrecht, and Tournai the cathedral chapters no doubt exercised a similar influence.

wooden houses by more durable constructions in brick or stone. Art craftsmen soon found that to be able to work in peace it was no longer necessary to remain under the shadow of the abbeys, and numbers of them removed into the towns. There they quickly discovered that their position as independent craftsmen was anything but stable, and that to succeed they must unite with one or other of the existing industrial corporations. So in many towns the masons and sculptors joined that of the carpenters; the painters and glass-painters that of the saddlers and glaziers. All these corporations, primarily formed to protect and further the temporal interests of their members, had also a religious side, the members being bound to join and subscribe to the guild in honour of the saint chosen as patron of the corporation. During the thirteenth century some few monasteries, such as the Cistercian abbey of the Dunes near Furnes, and the Benedictine abbey of S. Hubert in the Ardennes, still kept a body of art craftsmen about them, but these gradually diminished in number, and from the close of the century the arts only flourished and progressed in the towns in which those who practised them formed part of a chartered corporation. No man practising a craft already in the possession of a chartered corporation could work for pay in a town unless he were a burgher by birth or by purchase, and a member of that corporation. As such he obtained a recognised position, but was also subject to strictly enforced regulations. Painters neither looked on themselves nor were considered by the public as superior to other craftsmen. It was not until art began to decay that they gave themselves superior airs. During the great ages they were paid for their work like other craftsmen; it had to be good, honest work executed with good materials—the officers of the corporation saw to that—and it was each man's aim to make his work as beautiful as he could. The old warning, *Caveat emptor*, as regards the works executed by members of the chartered art corporations, became obsolete, and attention to it only again became necessary when sculptors and painters emancipated themselves from all control save that of the law courts, quite incompetent to deal with such matters. The corporation took care to secure the proper training of its members. A lad had to be bound apprentice for a term of years to a master painter, who became responsible for his technical education, and for his attention to his religious duties. The boy lived with his master, served him and had to obey him; the master in return had to give him thorough instruction in all matters relating to his craft : how to prepare his panel or canvas, how to prepare and lay on the gesso ground, how to mix his colours and make his varnishes. His apprenticeship terminated, the youth became a journeyman, and could work for pay under any master he chose, either in his own town or elsewhere ; after a time he would present himself before the appointed officers of the corporation for admission to the rank of master painter. He was required to give satisfactory evidence of his technical knowledge and to execute a picture. He had next to take an oath to obey the laws of the corporation, and to promise that his work should be good and honest work in the sight of God. Then upon payment of certain fees, which varied in amount according to whether he were the son of a master painter or of an outsider, he became a full member of the corporation with a right to vote at the annual election of its officers, but though a free master, he remained all his life under the supervision of the inspectors of the corporation, who could at any time enter his shop and seize any materials that were bad, such as panels with knots in them and gold, silver, azure, or sinople of inferior quality ; these were confiscated and destroyed, and their owner fined. Again, if any dispute arose between a painter and his employer, the officers of the corporation were called in to settle it, to appraise the value of the work and, in case of a previous contract, to state whether the agreement had been honestly fulfilled, and whether the work delivered was executed according to contract. The painter of any scamped or dishonest work would be brought before the magistrates and severely punished. If, on the other hand, the work was found to be better than that contracted for, the complaining purchaser had to pay the difference between the price agreed upon and the real value, as also all the costs of the expert witnesses, &c. The art corporations grew in power during the fourteenth century, but did not attain their full importance until towards the middle of the fifteenth. At that time delegates from all the chartered corporations of painters throughout the Low Countries met every third year in one or other town, where they spent several days in discussing matters of common interest and in communicating to one another the discovery of improvements in technical methods. These periodical reunions fully explain the remarkable uniformity in the processes employed throughout the Low Countries and prove that until the middle of the sixteenth century there was really only one school, the old and proper name of which is the Early Netherlandish, and not the Early Flemish school, for so far as our present knowledge goes, Flanders during the whole of the fifteenth century gave birth to very few painters of any great merit, and the most distinguished of these were sons of Dutchmen.

I will now endeavour to give, in the limited space at my disposal, a brief sketch of the history of the Netherlandish school from the commencement of the thirteenth century. At the very beginning of that glorious epoch Wolfram von Eschenbach, in a poem which was written before 1215, mentions Maastricht and Coeln as the two cities in which the art of painting had risen to distinction. We have documentary evidence of the execution of many fine mural paintings during this and the two following centuries; others have been brought to light in recent years. The earliest known portable paintings are those adorning the wooden shrine of Saint Odilia, one of the companions of Saint Ursula, which was painted in 1292 at Huy or at Liége, and discovered by me in October 1863.[1] These represent a series of scenes in her life, painted on plain red or green backgrounds; the compositions are simple and tell their story well; the drawing is good; the figures are, however, somewhat short, a feature which is also a marked characteristic of painters of the Mosan country in later times. The next pictures in point of date that have come down to us are : 1. a panel representing Henry von Rhijn, archdeacon of Utrecht (died 1360) kneeling at the feet of Christ on the Cross, the Blessed Virgin and S. John, on a ground of gold burnished and tooled; the portrait is wanting in individual character and the modelling of the figures weak (now in the Museum at Antwerp). 2. A Calvary picture with SS. Barbara and Katherine, painted c. 1390, for the Corporation of Tanners of Bruges, now in the cathedral; this, also on a tooled gold background, is a better picture; the figure of the Blessed Virgin, who is supported by two holy women, is very noble, and the heads of several of the figures are animated. 3. The shutters of a carved altar reredos executed for the Charterhouse of Dijon by Melchior Broederlam of Ipres, the official painter of Philip, Duke of Burgundy, from 1382 to 1401. The subjects represented are the Annunciation, Visitation, Presentation, and Flight into Egypt, treated in a very different manner to the foregoing, the figures being individualised

---

[1] An excellent illustrated description of these, by Mr. J. Helbig, will be found in "Le Beffroi," vol. ii, pp. 31—37, Bruges, 1864.

and showing a delicate feeling for beauty, the colouring clear and intense; buildings, castle-crowned rocks and trees of conventional character are introduced, but
the sky is replaced by a gold ground.[1]

The fifteenth century witnessed an immense development in Netherlandish
pictorial art; this was owing to the discovery of the Van Eycks, natives of
Maaseyck, a small town on the River Maas, below Maastricht. The best au-
thorities are generally agreed that Hubert van Eyck was born about 1370, and
John about 1390, and that their discovery of a new process of painting in oil was
made before 1415. Of course, oil painting had long been in use, certainly from
the twelfth century, as Theophilus describes the process, but only in an unde-
veloped form, and for inferior purposes. No doubt slight improvements were
made, and it is quite possible that a partial use of oil was made in some panel pictures, such as those by Broederlam at Dijon. But any way, the simplification and
perfecting of the process was due to the Van Eycks. Their discovery brought
about a great change. Hitherto, Painting had been subservient to Architecture,
but now it began to be independent. Instead of being confined to the ornamentation of the surface of walls, its aim would be to create illusion and by the perfecting of linear and aerial perspective to make the spectator forget the existence
of a flat surface. It thus became a direct imitator, or by idealisation a rival
of nature.

It is not known where or from whom the Van Eycks learnt their art, possibly
at Coeln. Several pictures by Hubert are mentioned in contemporary documents,
but the only example which can be ascribed to him, and that only in part, is the
celebrated altar-piece of the Adoration of the Lamb. It is not even known when
Hubert went to Ghent, probably not before 1420;[2] he certainly settled there in or

---

[1] Now in the Museum at Dijon. Outline sketches of these will be found in WAAGEN,
"Handbook of Painting," part I, p. 39, London, 1860; and in CROWE and CAVALCASELLE,
"The Early Flemish Painters," 2nd edition, p. 24, London, 1872.

[2] The so-called Register of the Corporation of Painters and Sculptors of Ghent and the
Rhymed Biography of Netherlandish Painters, attributed to Luke de Heere, published with
annotations by Mr. E. de Busscher in a volume entitled "Recherches sur les Peintres
Gantois," the documents relating to the Van Eycks said to have been discovered by
Mr. Van Kirckhoff at Antwerp, and by Mr. Schellinck at Ghent, the authenticity of which I

before 1424, and died there on the 18th of September, 1426, leaving the altar-piece unfinished.

Of the earlier years of John van Eyck's life we have no record. A signed picture, dated 30 October, 1421, representing the enthronement of S. Thomas of Canterbury, and said to have been given to Henry VI. by his uncle, the Duke of Bedford, is the earliest piece of evidence yet discovered.[1]

His first known patron was John of Bavaria, who took him into his service as painter and chamberlain, probably in 1420 or 1421. He was employed at the Hague in the decoration of his palace from 24 October, 1422, to 11 September, 1424. In 1425 he was at Bruges and entered the service of Philip, Duke of Burgundy, on the 19th of May. In August he removed to Lille. In 1426 he was sent on two secret missions by the Duke. In 1428 he was sent in the suite of John, lord of Roubaix, to Portugal to paint the portrait of the Infanta Isabel. They started from Bruges on the 19th of October, put in at Sandwich on the next day, sailed thence on the 13th of November, put in at Falmouth on the 25th, set sail again on December 2nd, and arrived at Lisbon on the 18th. After a short stay they rode to Arrayollos, and thence on the 12th of January to Aviz. On the morrow they were received at Court. John van Eyck painted the portrait of the princess, which towards the middle of February was sent to Duke Philip, together with the preliminaries of a marriage treaty. While waiting for the Duke's reply they went first on a pilgrimage to the shrine of S. James at Compostella, then visited John II., king of Castile, the Duke of Arjona in Andalusia, and Mahomet, the Moorish king of Granada. They then returned through Andalusia to Lisbon. Philip's consent having arrived, they went on June 4th to the court at Cintra. The marriage by proxy was celebrated in July. On the 8th of October the Portuguese fleet, with the bridal party, set sail. They encountered bad weather, were compelled to put in at different harbours, and only reached Sluus on Christmas Day.[2]

was the first to question ("*Notes sur Jean van Eyck*," 1861, p. 34 ; "*Le Beffroi*," vol. ii. pp. 207, 208, 212 and 213, Bruges, 1864), are now proved to be impudent forgeries.

[1] Now at Chatsworth ; unfortunately almost entirely overpainted.

[2] The account of the voyage, written in French by a member of the mission, from which these notes are taken, will be found in GACHARD, "*Collection de documents inédits*," vol. ii. pp. 63-91, Brussels, 1834.

There can be little doubt that during his sojourn at the Hague, Van Eyck must have exercised a considerable influence on the painters of Haarlem and other neighbouring towns, and during his travels in the Peninsula the new method of painting will have become widely known. Doubtless, too, he may have presented specimens of his art to, or received commissions from, some of the sovereigns whose courts he visited.

John van Eyck, never at a higher level as regards conception and choice of types than when working under the influence of Hubert, became more realistic after 1432, the saints in his pictures and even the figures of the Infant Christ and His Virgin Mother being only too faithful portraits of ill-chosen models. As a realistic portrait painter he has never been surpassed, while his landscape backgrounds with their wonderfully delicate modulations of atmosphere long remained unequalled. Above all he was remarkable for the consummate skill with which he reproduced the most minute details, for the care displayed by him in the choice of materials and the excellence of his methods of execution. Our National Gallery contains three of his masterpieces.

The only master known to have been trained by him is Peter Christus, a native of Baerle, near Tilburg, in North Brabant, who settled in Bruges, and died there in 1470. His earliest work is a portrait of Edward Grimston in the possession of Lord Verulam; his best work the Saints Eligius and Godeberta, 1449, in the Oppenheim Collection at Coeln, both signed.

I will now endeavour to show where the principal masters of the school whose works have come down to us were born and received their art training. The painters of Haarlem early rose to eminence; they were especially distinguished for their landscape backgrounds, and for the skilful rendering of draperies. The earliest of these, Albert Van Ouwater, was still living in 1467; the Berlin Museum possesses the only known picture proved to be by him, the Raising of Lazarus. By his pupil, Gerard of Saint John, who died at the age of twenty-eight, we have two pictures, one representing the dead Christ on the lap of His Mother, with other figures around; the other, scenes from the legend of Saint John the Baptist. Dirk Bouts, who settled in Louvain before 1449, was the son of a Haarlem painter of the same name, and no doubt learnt his craft in that city. His principal works executed for the Town-hall and the church of Louvain are now partly in the latter, partly in the museums of Brussels, Munich, and Berlin. Our National Gallery possesses his portrait painted in 1462.

Ghent is generally said to have given birth to Hugh van der Goes, but the documents alleged to prove this are now known to be modern forgeries. In all probability he was a native of Ter Goes, in Zealand, who settled in Ghent about 1465, and resided there and at Bruges until 1476, when, following the example of his brother, he entered the monastery of the Austin Canons at Roodenclooster in Brabant as a lay brother ; he died there in 1482. The only work by him, the authenticity of which is established, is the altar-piece executed for Thomas Portunari, the agent of the Medici at Bruges, and given by him to the Hospital of Santa Maria Nuova at Florence. As a composition it is rather weak, but the portraits of the donors and their children are excellent, full of individual character ; these and the figures of the shepherds are evidently true to nature. He was certainly influenced by John van Eyck in a greater degree than any other master of the school.[1]

Tournai, a cathedral town, in which the arts had flourished from an early date, was the native place of a painter who exercised an even wider influence than Van Eyck, Roger de la Pasture, better known as Van der Weyden, the exact Flemish equivalent of his family name. He had been for more than five years the pupil of Robert Campin when he was admitted as master into the Guild of Saint Luke on 1st August, 1432. He removed to Brussels in or before 1435, and was appointed painter in ordinary of that town in 1436. In 1449 he went on a pilgrimage to Rome, and, amongst other cities, visited Ferrara. He died in Brussels in 1464. He was evidently a far more religious man than Van Eyck. His figures are less naturalistic and the arrangement of them more dramatic. He put more animation into them, and apparently was always striving to express the tenderness, the compassion, the grief which he himself felt when meditating on the subjects he was representing. Of the numerous paintings of very different kinds of workmanship attributed to him, many must be by other artists. The following, however, are of undoubted authenticity. A triptych, formerly in the Charter-house of Miraflores, near Burgos ; the altar-piece of the Church of Middelburg,

---

[1] For the altar of the Portunari family, in the Church of Saint James, at Bruges, he painted a large picture of the Taking down from the Cross, which has been lost sight of since 1783.

near Bruges, painted for Peter Bladelin, both now at Berlin ; a Madonna, with
SS. Peter and John, Cosmas and Damian, painted for Cosmo dei Medici, now at
Frankfort ; the Descent from the Cross, formerly in the Chapel of Our Lady
without the walls of Louvain, now at Madrid ; and the life-size figures of Christ
on the Cross, with the Blessed Virgin and S. John, painted for the Charterhouse
at Scheut, near Brussels, now in the Escurial.

Germany gave birth to another master who has attained world-wide celebrity,
Hans Memlinc, who derived his name either from the village of Mümling, near
Aschaffenburg, or that of Memelinc, in North Holland.   He was, however, born
in the diocese of Mentz, and learnt his art in that city or at Coeln.   His apprenticeship being ended, he came to the Low Countries, and most probably worked
as a journeyman under Roger Van der Weyden.   He settled finally at Bruges
some time before 1478, probably in 1471, if not still earlier, and there died on the
11th of August, 1494.   Memlinc was evidently a religious man like Van der
Weyden, but of a different type of character, humble and affectionate, a lover of
peace, of a poetical, and perhaps even of a sentimental turn of mind.   His pictures
reflect this, being distinguished by their pure feeling, their grace of outline and
their harmony of colour.   They may best be described as idylls.   It is, however,
by the portraits they executed that the particular genius and the technical powers
of the different masters of the school can best be appraised, and if one were to
judge by the portraits Memlinc painted, one would conclude that his patrons
were almost exclusively pious, honest folk, which can hardly have been the case.
In a few instances, such as in the likenesses of the banker and burgomaster,
William Moreel, he has succeeded in conveying the idea of an able man with a
strong will, but he knew this man well.   He was far more successful in his
portraiture of children, and was the first master of the school who could paint
a baby.

His authentic pictures are numerous ; his earliest work, a triptych now at
Chatsworth, painted for Sir John Donne, must have been executed between 1461
and July, 1469, probably at Bruges in 1468 ; the landscape in this picture bears
considerable resemblance to that in his portrait of the Italian medallist, Nicolas
Spinelli, painted in 1468, now in the Antwerp museum.   An altar-piece now at
Turin, representing the incidents in the Passion of Our Lord in a number of little

pictures artificially separated from each other by buildings, walls, rocks or hillocks, given to the Guild of Stationers at Bruges by the miniaturist William Vrelant and his wife, was painted before 1478. A similarly treated and even finer picture represents twenty-eight scenes in the life of Christ and the Blessed Virgin in all of which, it seems to me, the painter, inspired by the contemplation of Christ as the Light of the World, sought to express the revelation of the Divinity made through the Incarnation. This was given to the Corporation of Tanners of Bruges, in 1480, and is now at Munich. In both of these the donors are represented kneeling in the foreground. The well-known large altar-piece of S. John's Hospital, and the triptych representing the Adoration of the Magi, the Nativity and Presentation with the kneeling figure of Brother John Floreins, are dated 1479 ; the altar-piece of the Moreel chantry in the church of S. James, 1484 ; the diptych with half-length figures of the Blessed Virgin and Martin van Nieuwenhove, 1487 ; and the shrine of S. Ursula finished in 1489 ; all still in Bruges. The Madonna with kneeling figures of James Floreins, a merchant of Bruges, his wife and their numerous children protected by their patron saints, painted before 1488 ; a diptych, one panel of which represents the Madonna surrounded by six virgin Saints ; the other, the donor John Du Celier protected by S. John Baptist, with S. John's vision in the isle of Patmos and S. George slaying the dragon in the background ; and two wings with SS. John Baptist and Mary Magdalene, all in the Louvre, are also noteworthy. Our National Gallery possesses one small panel, the Blessed Virgin and Child with the donor protected by S. George ; this has unfortunately been injured in part by rubbing.

Another artist of German origin who settled at s'Hertoghen Bossche, and is generally known as Jerome Bosch (c. 1460—1516), and as the painter of fantastic demoniacal scenes, was really a master of great power who followed the early technical processes. His finest pictures are in the Prado Gallery at Madrid ; there is also in the Museum at Bruges a delicately painted Adoration of the Magi by him.

Oudewater in South Holland was the birth-place of Gerard, son of John David, who probably learnt the art of painting either at Haarlem or from Dirk Bouts. He came to Bruges at the end of 1483, or at the commencement of 1484, and was admitted as master-painter into the Guild of S. Luke on the 14th of January.

B

The Museum at Bruges possesses two panels representing the Judgment of Cambyses and the Flaying of the Unjust Judge, commenced in 1488 and terminated in 1498 ; and a triptych representing the Baptism of Christ, with the donor and his first wife, their children and patron saints on the interior of the shutters, and his second wife and her first-born daughter, protected by S. Mary Magdalene, kneeling before Our Lady and Child on the interior ; the former painted before 1502, the latter before 1508. David's masterpiece, however, now in the Museum at Rouen, was presented by him in 1500 to the Carmelite nuns of Sion at Bruges. It represents the Blessed Virgin and Child with two lovely angels, ten virgin saints and the painter and his wife. Our National Gallery possesses two fine works, painted about 1501, both formerly in the Cathedral at Bruges. The two first mentioned panels bear the impress of his Dutch training ; the brilliant colouring and the gloss and polish of his pictures remind one of Bouts. His later pictures show the influence of Memlinc's softer and more delicate manner. His saints are graceful and poetical, but often untrue to their character. His Madonnas are of an intellectual and dignified type, but a little cold when compared with those of Memlinc, whom, however, he surpassed in the representation of the Holy Child. David was also an excellent miniaturist, and as such was at the head of a school of miniature painters and illuminators which flourished at Bruges ; his wife and daughter excelled in the same art.

The only painter who can be said with certainty to have been trained by David is Adrian Isenbrant. We do not know where he served his apprenticeship ; he came to Bruges as a journeyman. In 1510 he purchased the right of citizenship, and was admitted as free master into the Guild of S. Luke. He painted for the Church of S. Basil at Bruges an altar-piece representing the Marriage Feast at Cana, which was completed in 1523 or early in 1524. It is painted with great body of colour ; the type of the figures and general arrangement of the composition are very like David's work, but the sharp contrasts of brilliant colours in the dresses exceed anything in his pictures. The portraits of the donor and his family are excellent.

David's earlier pictures are remarkable for the beauty of their landscape backgrounds, evidently careful studies of scenery in the district between the Meuse and the Rhine. In these he was probably assisted by Joachim Patenir of Dinant, who accompanied him to Antwerp in 1515, when they were both made free of the local guild as master painters. Patenir settled there, and during the remaining nine years of his life painted a large number of landscapes, some of which are strikingly like those in the backgrounds of David's pictures. The figures in these are often the work of other artists.

Henry Bles, of Bouvignes—a town on the Meuse opposite Dinant—was also a clever landscapist, but his colouring is cooler. He was in the habit of introducing an owl amid the foliage in his pictures, and this procured him the nickname of Civetta in Italy, where his paintings were greatly prized.

Louvain gave birth in 1466 to Quentin Metsys, who afterwards settled in Antwerp, where he continued to reside until his death in 1530. His earlier pictures are remarkable for the clearness of their colour, the delicacy of features, and the skilful care with which they are finished. His two most important works of this class are the altar-piece of the Joiners' Guild of Antwerp, now in the Museum of that city, and the family of S. Anne, formerly in S. Peter's at Louvain, now at Brussels. In our National Gallery are two fine heads of Christ and the Blessed Virgin, of wonderfully delicate feeling and expression. Replicas of these are in the Antwerp Museum. Metsys was the last of the old school of religious painters at Antwerp. He is perhaps more widely known as the painter of pictures representing money-changers, receivers of municipal taxes; by far the greater number of these, however, are by his son, John Metsys, Marinus of Remerswal, and Cornelius van der Capelle, who afterwards settled in Lyons and was celebrated for his portraits.

Leyden was the birthplace of Cornelius Engelbrechtsen, 1468—1533, whose only authentic picture is an altar-piece in the Town Hall of that city. His pupil, Luke Huigensz, 1494—1533, was a talented artist who drew and engraved admirably. His paintings are poor as compositions and wanting in religious feeling, but his scenes from common life are evidently true to nature.

John Gossaert, a native of Maubeuge, was born about 1470. We do not know where he learnt the technique of his art, but he unquestionably learnt it thoroughly. His earlier pictures, apparently based on the study of Memlinc and Gerard David's works, are remarkable for the warmth of their colour and the skilful rendering of the minutest detail of costume, but they are wanting in religious feeling. His principal work of this period is an Adoration of the Magi in the possession of the Earl of Carlisle. He went to Italy in 1512, and was evidently so captivated by the Renascence that he threw off the traditions of his native style. After that his pictures of religious subjects are only remarkable for their masterly modelling and vigorous colouring, and for the richness of their architectural accessories. On the other hand his portraits are very fine.

Another painter of the transition period is Bernard Van Orley, a native of Brussels, 1471—1541, who in Italy devoted himself to the study of Raphael. His pictures are ably composed, and his figures show more feeling and taste than those by Gossaert. The execution is remarkably careful. Our Lady of Dolours, with portraits of donors on the shutters, is a fine work, as is also the History of Job, both in the Museum at Brussels.

Two other masters who settled in Bruges, Lancelot Blondeel of Poperinghe, 1496—1561, and Peter Pourbus of Gouda (c. 1510—1584), must also be mentioned in this category. The former was the designer of the chimney-piece in the Council Hall of the Liberty of Bruges, of which there is a cast at South Kensington, and of many monuments in the Renascence style, and was a careful painter of religious subjects, which he generally surrounded with rich architectural work, executed in brown varnish on a gold ground. His best works are still at Bruges; the finest, dated 1545, painted for the Corporation of Saddlers and Painters, represents the Madonna with SS. Eligius and Luke. His son-in-law, Peter Pourbus, had studied in Italy before settling in Bruges; he was a man of multifarious powers and prodigious activity. It is noteworthy that he was captivated by the beauty of the old masters, and was never tired of gazing on the works of Memlinc and David. There are some fifteenth century pictures in Bruges to which he added wings that are not out of harmony with them. His picture of Our Lady of Dolours in the Church of S. James, dated 1556, was evidently inspired by an earlier painting in the Church of Our Lady. He was also very successful as a portrait painter, a branch of the art which was carried on by his son at Antwerp and by his grandson in France.

In no town did the traditions of the old school find followers longer than in Bruges. Peter Claeis the elder was a painter and illuminator who settled in Bruges early in the sixteenth century, and he seems to have worked under Gerard

David ; his sons and grandsons followed in his footsteps ; the latest work of one of the latter is an altar-piece painted for the Confraternity of Our Lady of the Dry Tree in the Church of S. Walburg, ordered in 1606, but not completed until 1620.

This sketch, necessarily brief and imperfect, has been written to give those who have not studied the works of the Early School some idea of its rise and of the different influences that shared in its development. Those who wish to become better acquainted with its history would do well to read Crowe and Cavalcaselle's "Early Flemish Painters," 2nd Edition, 1872, and Sir W. M. Conway's "Early Flemish Artists," 1887. These are the latest English works on the subject. Many monographs and notices have, however, appeared since then in Germany, Holland, and Belgium, some of which throw fresh light on the subject.

W. H. WEALE.

CATALOGUE

The works are catalogued under the names given to them by the Contributors. The Directors cannot be responsible for the attributions.
The Numbers commence in the West Room, and continue from left to right.
Throughout the Catalogue, in describing the pictures, the RIGHT *and* LEFT *mean those of the spectator facing the picture.*

WEST ROOM.

WORKS OF THE EARLY FLEMISH OR NETHERLANDISH SCHOOL.

1. THE VIRGIN AND CHILD AND THE CRUCIFIXION. A Diptych.

> One volet, showing the Virgin and Child enthroned ; the other, the Crucifixion, against a background of gold, highly embossed. Panel (each), 16 × 10 in.

EARLY SCHOOL OF COLOGNE. Lent by SIR CHARLES ROBINSON.

2. THE VIRGIN AND CHILD ENTHRONED.

> The Virgin crowned, seated facing, within a porch of Gothic style, and dressed in a blue robe lined with fur, supports the Child with her right hand, and with her left offers Him her breast ; His dress is red ; at the foot of the wall on either side of the porch are plants in flower. Panel, 5¾ × 4 in. From the collections of Frederick II. of Prussia, of Aders and Samuel Rogers.
> This picture has been ascribed to Van Eyck and to Memlinc. See *Catalogue of the Northbrook Collection*, No. 1.

By ROGIER VAN DER WEYDEN. Lent by the EARL OF NORTHBROOK, K.C.I.E.

3. THE ADORATION OF THE MAGI, THE VIRGIN AND CHILD AND
THE DESCENT OF THE HOLY GHOST. A Triptych.

> In the centre compartment before a lofty building is depicted the adoration of the Magi ; on a balcony with steps leading to it are numerous figures, one holding a banner ; the Star of Bethlehem is seen in the sky in the distance ; on the left panel, the Virgin and Child in a mandorla ; beneath, a landscape ; on the right panel, the Descent of the Holy Ghost ; the disciples are assembled in the upper room with the Virgin seated in the foreground, reading. Panel, centre, 15 × 9¾ in. ; sides, 15 × 4¼ in.

Hitherto ascribed to JAN GOSSAERT, called MABUSE.

Lent by SIR FRANCIS COOK, BART.

4. THE CRUCIFIXION AND THE ENTOMBMENT.

Christ on the cross, at the foot of which kneels St. Mary Magdalene ; her right arm encircles the cross ; her left rests on a vase, near which is a skull ; on the left stand the Virgin and St. John ; in the background is seen the entombment. Panel, 6¾ × 4½ in.

By PEDRO CAMPANA.   Lent by SIR FRANCIS COOK, BART.

5. THE CONVERSION OF ST. PAUL, AND ST. CATHERINE. A Diptych.

On the left panel St. Paul falling from his horse, which stumbles forwards, and looking up at the Saviour who appears in the clouds ; on the ground lie his hat and a parchment with seal ; on the right panel St. Catherine standing facing on the back of a prostrate king, Maximin, who grasps his sceptre with his right hand ; the Saint rests her left hand on her sword, and is attired in a dress with red skirt and pale green bodice and blue sleeves ; on her head a crown ; at her feet is the broken spiked wheel. The scenes are each depicted through an archway. Panel, 7½ × 4½ in. each.

By BERNARD VAN ORLEY.   Lent by SIR FRANCIS COOK, BART.

6. THE VIRGIN AND CHILD.

Three-quarter length figure of the Virgin seated towards left, the Child on her knees ; her left arm rests on a carved ledge, on which is a vase and before which is an apple ; with her right she supports the Child, Who holds cherries in each hand ; the Virgin is robed in a red dress and blue, gold-lined mantle ; on her head a lilac velvet cap ; curtain and architectural background ; through a window on the left is seen a landscape with reapers. Panel, 27½ × 20 in.

By JAN GOSSAERT, called MABUSE.   Lent by SIR FRANCIS COOK, BART.

7. THE VIRGIN AND CHILD AND ANGELS.

Within a chamber the Virgin is seated, facing, at the fireside ; she wears green dress and red flowing mantle, and has white drapery on her head ; the Child, lying across her knees, is looking up at His mother ; on the right are three angels chanting, and behind them a high canopied bed ; on the left is seen another angel approaching through a doorway and bearing food for the Infant Jesus. Panel, 32½ × 21¾ in.

EARLY FLEMISH SCHOOL.   Lent by SIR FRANCIS COOK, BART.

8. ST. CATHERINE DISPUTING WITH THE PHILOSOPHERS. A Triptych.

In the centre within a portico, and in front of an alcove, before which hangs a brown curtain, stands St. Catherine facing, reading from a book which she holds in her left hand, her right resting on her sword : she is crowned, and wears a pink dress and blue mantle, and a brown girdle ; at her feet lies another book, partly open ; on the right and left and through the portico are seen the sages and philosophers, singly or in groups, mostly seated, consulting their books ; on the left panel are three other sages consulting a book, which lies open on the knees of the central figure ; on the right panel is the tyrant Maximin on his throne, his sceptre in his left hand, and addressing a man who is seated near him, his hands crossed on his breast ; through the pillars of the portico, in each compartment, are seen the town of Alexandria and the surrounding country ; the frieze of the portico is decorated with scenes from the life of St. Catherine. Panel, centre, 43 × 33¾ in ; sides, 43 × 14½ in.

By JAN GOSSAERT, called MABUSE.   Lent by SIR FRANCIS COOK, BART.

9. THE HOLY WOMEN AT THE SEPULCHRE.

In the centre, the empty tomb of Christ, an angel in white robes seated on the displaced lid ; on the left the three Marys, bearing boxes of ointment ; to the right and in the foreground the sleeping guards ; in the middle distance a green mound, probably representing the Mount of Olives, and a road, on which horsemen are returning to Jerusalem ; right and left, cliffs of brown rock ; across the background the houses and towers of Jerusalem, a conspicuous object in the midst being the mosque of Omar, intended for the Temple ; in the foreground, plants. In the right-hand corner is a coat of arms. Panel, 28⅛ × 34¾ in.

The analogy is striking between some parts of this picture, especially the angel seated on the tomb, and those parts of the Ghent altar-piece (*The Adoration of the Lamb*, in St. Bavon), generally accepted as the work of Hubert van Eyck.

By JAN VAN EYCK.   Lent by SIR FRANCIS COOK, BART.

10. THE VIRGIN AND CHILD AND ANGELS.

Small three-quarter length figure of the Virgin, seated facing, in blue dress, red mantle and white veil ; she holds in her arms the Infant Jesus, Who turning away receives a bunch of grapes from an angel ; He is placing a grape in His mouth ; on the right stands another angel playing on a lute ; before, on a parapet, are a book, a vase with flowers, and an apple ; in the background, landscape. Panel, 16¼ × 11½ in.

Attributed to GHEERAERT DAVID.   Lent by SIR FRANCIS COOK, BART.

11. THE VIRGIN AND CHILD AND SAINTS.

The Virgin holding the Child on her right arm, stands before an altar in a church ; she offers Him an apple with her left hand ; above, an angel holding a crown. On the left of the altar are St. John and St. Peter, and on the right St. Damian and St. Cosmas, one holding a spatula and a pot, the other a vial, his left hand being placed on an open book. Panel, 18 × 12¼ in.

By ROGIER VAN DER WEYDEN.   Lent by SIR FRANCIS COOK, BART.

12. HERCULES AND OMPHALE.

Two nude figures seated in an alcove of grey stone ; Hercules holds a spiked club in his right hand, and with his left embraces Omphale. Dated "151" on a flag-stone to the left. Panel, 12¼ × 10⅞ in.

By JAN GOSSAERT, called MABUSE.   Lent by SIR FRANCIS COOK, BART.

13. THE SELECTION OF ST. JOSEPH FROM AMONG THE SUITORS FOR THE HAND OF THE VIRGIN, AND THE NATIVITY. (In the centre of the room.)

Two pictures painted on one panel :—

1. Within the Temple the High Priest standing before the altar ; before him, and on the left of the altar, are the suitors holding their wands ; in the midst of them is St. Joseph, whose wand has blossomed ; the High Priest grasps the robe of St. Joseph and draws attention to his rod ; in the foreground, a dog.

2. In the centre of the picture lies the Holy Child in a manger, around which kneel three angels and the Virgin ; behind the Virgin stands St. Joseph with a lantern ; above the group hovers another angel ; on the right, through an arch, is seen two men, one of whom holds a lute and the other points to the Child ; and in the distance a ruined house with fire and the shepherds watching their flocks ; above, on the arch, is seated an owl, said to be the private mark of the painter, by which he was known as " Civetta."   Panel, 53½ × 54¼ in.

The centrepiece of a triptych, painted back and front, of which the side volets are lost.

Probably by HERRI DE BLES (CIVETTA).   Lent by SIR FRANCIS COOK, BART.

14. THE CRUCIFIXION AND ST. JEROME AND ST. FRANCIS. A Triptych.

In the centre panel Christ crucified ; on the left of the Cross stands the Holy Virgin, and on the right St. John ; on the right panel St. Jerome in prayer, and on the left one St. Francis, who is receiving the stigmata.   On the reverse of the panels, a view of Jerusalem, with the Cross in the foreground.   Panel, centre, 10¾ × 7½ in. ; sides, 11½ × 3¾.

By JOACHIM PATINIR.   Lent by ALFRED STOWE, ESQ.

15. SCENES FROM THE PASSION.

The composition is divided into four square compartments by a painted framing of Gothic architecture.

1. In the upper register, on the left, is the Garden of Gethsemane, with the sleeping disciples, and Christ kneeling before a chalice, above which is a consecrated wafer ; Judas and soldiers in the background.

2. Christ, falling under His cross, is struck by a soldier ; St. Veronica, kneeling before Him, holds the veil on which is the impress of His face ; Simon of Cyrene supports the cross ; in the background, the Holy Women, the two thieves, priests, Jews, and others.

3. The Crucifixion ; on the left is the Virgin, and on the right, St. John ; the Magdalene embraces the feet of Christ.

4. The Deposition ; the Virgin and St. John support the dead Christ ; the Magdalene and holy women kneel behind ; in the background the tomb, with Joseph of Arimathea and the disciples.   Panel, 11½ × 11 in.

From the Collection of Señor Benito Garriga of Madrid.

EARLY FLEMISH SCHOOL.   Lent by M. LÉON DE SOMZÉE.

16. ST. ENGRACIA. VIRGIN AND MARTYR.

Full length figure of the Saint, standing towards left, in front of a throne, habited in gold ermin-lined robe, over red velvet dress, and blue velvet mantle with richly embroidered and jewelled edge ; jewelled head-dress surmounted by a crown ; around her neck a gold linked chain ; in her right hand, she holds a palm, and in her left a nail ; her left shoe is inscribed IREM NOV. Panel, 64 × 28½ in. From the Court of Sarragossa.

St. Engracia, of Sarragossa, a Virgin, was martyred by being nailed to a post ; after death she was crowned by an angel.

EARLY FLEMISH SCHOOL.   Lent by M. LÉON DE SOMZÉE.

17. THE VISITATION AND THE PRESENTATION IN THE TEMPLE.

On two panels ; on the left panel is seen St. Elizabeth greeting the Virgin ; in the background St. Joseph approaching, and buildings with landscape ; on the right panel, the Virgin presenting the Child to Simeon in the Temple ; on her left St. Joseph, and behind her St. Elizabeth and Saint Anne ; on the inside of the panels are figures of St. Ildefonsus and St. Anthony of Padua. Panel, 18 × 12¾ in. each. From the Northwick Collection.

HUGO VAN DER GOES.   Lent by ANTONY GIBBS, ESQ.

18. THE TRIUMPH OF DEATH.

An allegorical scene ; on the left are Time and Fame fleeing ; and towards the centre is Death, who is shooting an arrow at a crowd of men and women of all classes, issuing through an archway of a city ; in the background another figure of Death is shooting at animals and beasts ; above in the air are birds ; in the foreground are books and implements of various kinds ; buildings seen in the background. Panel, 19½ × 26 in.

By DAVID VINCKEBOONS.   Lent by HUGH P. LANE, ESQ.

19. PILATE WASHING HIS HANDS.

On the left Pilate, seated on a throne, around which are a crowd of Jews and soldiers, is washing his hands in a golden basin ; besides this principal scene there are representations in the background of the *Ecce Homo*, the *Flagellation* and the *Crowning with Thorns*. Panel, 42 × 20 in. From the Roscoe Collection. Waagen, iii., p. 235.

By MICHAEL WOHLGEMUTH.

Lent by the TRUSTEES OF THE ROYAL INSTITUTION, LIVERPOOL.

20. HEAD OF CHRIST.

Head of Christ, facing in crimson robe, edged with jewels. Panel, arched top, 16½ × 10½ in.

By JAN VAN EYCK.   Lent by M. LÉON DE SOMZÉE.

21.   THE VIRGIN AND CHILD AND SAINTS.

In the centre the Virgin, draped in red, seated under a canopy, over which is a trellised vine ; on her lap is the Infant Jesus, Who gives a ring to St. Catherine, seated on the left ; behind her kneels the donor ; on the right is St. Barbara holding an open book ; on either side of the Virgin is an angel ; landscape with architecture in the background.   Panel, 27 × 29 in.

The principal figures in this picture are the same as those in the great picture at St. John's Hospital, Bruges.

By HANS MEMLINC.   Lent by G. F. BODLEY, ESQ., A.R.A.

22.   THE DESCENT FROM THE CROSS.   A Triptych.

In the centre compartment the disciples taking down the body of the Christ from the Cross, at the foot of which are grouped St. John, supporting the Blessed Virgin, and the other Holy women : on the left panel is the donor with St. John, and on the right panel the wife of the donor with her patron, St. Martha, with the dragon ; landscape background with view of Jerusalem ; coats of arms in the right and left top corners. Panel, arched tops, centre, 42 × 28 in., sides, 42 × 13 in.

EARLY FLEMISH SCHOOL.   Lent by JOHN HARDMAN, ESQ.

23.   ECCE HOMO.

At the top of a flight of steps leading down from a narrow door, Christ stands facing the spectator ; beside Him are two guards ; on the right, a window with three figures looking out ; at the foot of the steps a crowd of ten persons ; others are standing near the steps ; through a narrow archway on the left are two men conversing. Panel, 20 × 14 in.

EARLY FLEMISH SCHOOL   Lent by CHARLES T. D. CREWS, ESQ.

24.   THE BEHEADING OF ST. JOHN THE BAPTIST.

In the centre of the picture stands the executioner, whose back is turned to the spectator ; he is placing the decapitated head of St. John on a charger, held by the daughter of Herodias, behind whom stands her mother ; at the feet of the executioner lies the dead body of the Saint ; on the right are a high priest and a man and a woman ; in the background is a high building, through the doorway of which are seen Herod and others seated at a feast.   Panel (arched), 45½ × 26½ in.

EARLY FLEMISH SCHOOL.   Lent by SIR HENRY H. HOWORTH, K.C.I.E., M.P.

25.   THE HOLY FAMILY AND ANGELS.

Within a chamber, the Virgin, seated under a canopy, supports the Infant Child on her knee, and places her hand on her breast ; the Child raises His right hand in the act of benediction, and holds the orb in His left ; near them stand two angels, one of whom holds a dish of fruit ; the other plays on a lute ; behind the group is St. Joseph, his hat in his left hand ; in the foreground is a table, on which is a flute, and on the wall at the back hangs an inscribed tablet ; through an opening on the right is seen a landscape. Panel 22 × 16 in.

EARLY FLEMISH SCHOOL.   Lent by the LORETO CONVENT, MANCHESTER.

26. THE VIRGIN AND CHILD AND SAINTS. A Triptych.

The Virgin in a blue dress, edged with gold lace, seated before a cloth of estate, within a portico ; she holds the Child, Who lies on her lap and is turning with His right hand the pages of a book, held by St. Barbara, in rich scarlet robe, and jewelled headdress ; an ostrich feather in her right hand ; on the right is seated St. Dorothy in a green robe, and having a flower in her right hand and a chaplet in her left ; a basket of flowers at her feet ; two angels on the right and left hold a sword and a lily ; in the background through the portico is seen a landscape with buildings ; on the left panel kneels the donor with his patron, St. John, standing behind him ; and on the right the wife of the donor with her patron, St. Catherine ; the two outside panels, originally outside the triptych, represent the Annunciation. Panel, centre, 34 × 28in.; sides each, 34 × 12 in.

By JACOB CORNELISSEN.   Lent by M. LÉON DE SOMZÉE.

27. ST. MARY MAGDALENE AND THE DONOR.

On the right stands St. Mary Magdalene in a richly embroidered red dress and green mantle, holding in her left hand the vase, and extending her right to the donor, who kneels at her side in prayer, and is robed in a brown velvet dress ; the jewelled head-dress of the Saint has the sacred monogram I.H.S. ; red curtain background. Panel, 21 × 14½ in. From the Ruston Collection.

By H. AND J. VAN EYCK.   Lent by M. LÉON DE SOMZÉE.

28. THE ADORATION OF THE MAGI. A Triptych.

In the centre the Adoration of the Magi ; the Virgin, holding the Child on her knees, is seated before a high arcade ; the Child is plunging His hand into a vase held by one of the Magi ; another stands on the left holding a sceptre and a vase ; through the arcade are seen a landscape and figures of soldiers and others ; on the left panel is an Eastern King with offerings ; and on the right St. Joseph, in blue coat and crimson mantle. Panel (arched top), centre 40½ × 26¼ in. ; sides 40½ × 10⅞ in.

By JAN VAN SCOREL.   Lent by SIR HENRY H. HOWORTH, K.C.I.E., M.P.

29. PORTRAIT OF A MAN.

Bust, turned slightly to the left of a stout man dressed in black coat with tippet of brown fur and black hat ; gold chain around his neck ; the figure is set against a stone archway, through which the sky is seen ; the hands rest on a stone ledge to the right. Panel (arched top), 24½ × 18½ in.

By JAN GOSSAERT, called MABUSE.   Lent by CAPTAIN G. L. HOLFORD, C.I.E.

30. MARY TUDOR, QUEEN OF LOUIS XII. OF FRANCE (1498–1533).
Daughter of Henry VII. ; married first (1514) Louis XII. of France, who died three
months after the marriage, and secondly, in secret, Charles Brandon, Duke of
Suffolk. The ceremony was publicly repeated soon after at Calais, and finally with
the consent of Henry VIII. at Greenwich, May 13, 1515.
Half-length figure, front, head turned slightly to left, in rich costume of gold
brocade, profusely ornamented with jewels and large pearls, necklace of pearls
with pendant ; bandeau of jewels on her head ; with both hands she holds a pot of
ointment, the emblem of St. Mary Magdalene, whom she is supposed to represent.
Panel (circular top), 16¼ × 12¾ in.

EARLY FLEMISH SCHOOL.   Lent by WICKHAM FLOWER, ESQ.

31. THE PIETY OF RAYMOND, COUNT OF TOULOUSE.
Deeply touched with the sense of his Saviour's suffering, the Count of Toulouse felt
himself unworthy to enjoy the luxuries and honours of his high station ; stripping
himself, therefore, of his dignities, he proceeded to the Holy Land in the garb of the
humblest pilgrim.
In the picture before us the Count is represented taking off his shirt, which a servant
in a brown-furred coat receives, who at the same time is holding the black-furred coat
which his master has laid aside, and which is partly on the ground. His cap lies there
also.   Next him stands the Bishop of Toulouse in his robes, wiping a tear from his
eye with his left hand, whilst with his right he partly covers the nakedness of the
Count with his robe. Next behind him are two other men, who are expressing their
sympathy at the scene. On the left in the middle distance through a gate is seen a
man bringing the pilgrim's dress, a short hair garment. On the right the Count
appears dressed in it, beginning his journey, the pilgrim's staff in his left hand, his
eyes cast up in humble aspiration, and the right hand on his breast. In the background, which consists of buildings and a piece of landscape, he appears again
attacked and beaten by robbers. Panel, 44½ × 32¾ in.
By some this picture is believed to represent St. Francis of Assisi renouncing the
world for the cloister.

By JOHN GOSSAERT called MABUSE.   Lent by R. C. SUTTON-NELTHORPE, ESQ.

32. A SHRINE OR RELIQUARY OF ST. NICHOLAS OF MYRA AND ST.
ANTHONY OF PADUA.
The subjects of the panels at the sides of the Shrine are as follows :—
1. St. Nicholas restoring to life the dismembered children in the salt tub.
2. Birth of St. Nicholas, Bishop of Myra.
3. St. Nicholas bestowing the dowry on the three daughters of a nobleman of
Panthera.
4. St. Anthony compelling a mule to kneel before the Holy Eucharist.
5. St. Anthony restoring to life a young child who was scalded to death, in the
presence of its parents.
6. St. Anthony preaching to the fishes.
On the ends of the shrine are figures in relief of St. Nicholas healing the
three dismembered children, and St. Anthony holding the Infant Jesus in
his arms.
From the collection of Cardinal Despuyg de Palma, Archbishop of Valencia.

By GHEEREART DAVID.   Lent by M. LÉON DE SOMZÉE.

33. MARGARET OF YORK, THIRD WIFE OF CHARLES THE BOLD, DUKE OF BURGUNDY (d. 1503).

Daughter of Richard Plantagenet, Duke of York, and sister of Edward IV. ; she was married in 1468 to Charles the Bold, Duke of Burgundy : died at Mechlin.

Bust, life-size, turned to left ; square cut crimson dress, trimmed with black velvet ; black head-dress ; around her neck a massive gold collar, ornamented with jewels, to which is attached a gold-linked chain with pendant, which passes over her shoulders. Panel, 18 × 13 in.

By HUGO VAN DER GOES.   Lent by the SOCIETY OF ANTIQUARIES.

34. MICHELE DE FRANCE, WIFE OF PHILIP LE BON, DUKE OF BURGUNDY AND DAUGHTER OF CHARLES VI. OF FRANCE AND ISABELLA DE BAVARIA. (See No. 59.)

Small half-length figure to left ; arms folded ; in crimson and gold-embroidered dress, lined with fur, high jewelled coif, with white veil.   Panel, 13½ × 10½ in.

EARLY FLEMISH SCHOOL.   Lent by GEORGE SALTING, ESQ.

35. ST. CATHERINE OF ALEXANDRIA.

Small three-quarter length figure of the Saint standing to right, grasping the hilt of her sword with her right hand, and holding in her left an open book, which she is reading ; pale blue robe, pink mantle, gold chain, and head-dress surmounted by a crown ; in the background on the right are a landscape and a castle on a hill.   Above on the left the Saint is seen kneeling before her wheel, her persecutors fleeing. Panel, 14½ × 10 in.

By HANS MEMLINC.   Lent by CHARLES BUTLER, ESQ.

36. THE VIRGIN AND CHILD.

Small full-length figure of the Virgin, seated under a tree in a landscape, suckling the Child, Who stands upon her lap encircled by her arms ; an open book lies on the ground at her feet ; in the background, landscape with river and castle.   Panel, 28 × 27 in.

By JAN GOSSAERT, called MABUSE.   Lent by JOHN G. WALLER, ESQ.

37. PATRICK ADAMSON, afterwards Archbishop of St. Andrews (1536–1592).

Born at Perth ; was educated at St. Andrews ; about 1569 became minister of Paisley, and in 1576 was raised to the Archiepiscopal See of St. Andrews.   He was antagonistic towards the Presbyterians, with whom he had many contests regarding the episcopacy.

Bust to left, under life size ; eyes turned to the spectator, black doublet, white ruff ; inscribed above, "PENSOSO D'AVTRVI ÆTATIS, 33 AN°, 1569." Panel, 17 × 12½ in.

By SIR ANTONIO MORE.   Lent by CHARLES BUTLER, ESQ.

38. PORTRAIT OF A LADY.

Half-length figure towards left, her hands crossed before her ; on a table lies an open book ; she wears black dress with red cape lined with white, white shirt and white cap ; gold necklet with pendant cross ; over her shoulders a massive gold chain attached to a jewelled girdle.   Panel, 17¼ × 11¾ in.

SCHOOL OF JAN VAN EYCK.   Lent by CHARLES BUTLER, ESQ.

39. THE VIRGIN AND CHILD AND ANGELS.

Small full-length figure of the Virgin seated, facing, beneath an arch decorated with figures ; she holds on her lap the Holy Child, who turning round, is receiving an apple from a kneeling angel, holding in his left hand a lute ; in the background, through the columns of the arch, is a landscape with buildings, and a rivulet in the foreground, near which stands an angel playing a lute.   Panel, 25¼ × 18½in.

By HANS MEMLINC.   Lent by the late DUKE OF WESTMINSTER, K.G.

40. PORTRAIT OF A LADY.

Small half-length figure turned to the left, chain of coral beads in her right hand ; her left is also shown ; black dress trimmed with white, white chemisette and cap.   Panel, 14½ × 10½ in.

By JACOB CORNELISSEN.   Lent by CHARLES T. D. CREWS, ESQ.

41. THE MAGDALENE.

Full length figure of the Magdalene standing to left and holding the golden vase in her hands ; brown square-cut dress, red sleeves and white cloak, embroidered at the hem ; around her neck a gold chain.   Panel, 21¾ × 9¾ in.

By HUGO VAN DER GOES.

Lent by the TRUSTEES OF THE ROYAL INSTITUTION, LIVERPOOL.

42. THE VIRGIN AND CHILD AND SAINTS.

Small full-length figure of the Virgin, seated on a low wall of a garden near a river and holding the Child on her lap ; with her left hand she is plucking a flower which grows on the wall ; behind her in the garden are three female saints walking, and in the background, city and river ; the First Person of the Trinity seen in the sky above.   Panel, 13½ × 9½ in.

By DIERICK BOUTS.   Lent by MRS. STEPHENSON CLARKE.

43. THE HOLY FAMILY.

The Virgin seated before a table on which stands the Holy Child, His hands resting on His mother's breast ; she supports the Child with her right hand, and with her left offers Him a flower ; on the table, which is partly covered by a cloth, are a glass

goblet containing wine, a cut orange, and a knife ; on the left St. Joseph, in a large straw hat, is reading a book ; landscape seen behind him. Panel, 20¾ × 15 in.
A somewhat similar picture, without landscape background, is in the National Gallery. It is lent by George Salting, Esq.

By THE MASTER OF "THE DEATH OF THE VIRGIN" (in the Munich Gallery).

Lent by FREDERICK L. COOK, ESQ., M.P.

44. ANNE OF CLEVES, QUEEN OF HENRY VIII. (1515–1557).

Half-length figure, turned towards left, habited in rich Flemish costume of gold tissue covered with jewellery, head-dress ornamented with pearls, and inscribed with the motto "A bon fine" ; in her right hand she holds a red carnation. Painted on vellum and strained on fine canvas, 15 × 14 in.
This portrait is supposed to have been executed by a Flemish painter a year or two previous to Anne's marriage in 1540.

EARLY FLEMISH SCHOOL. Lent by WICKHAM FLOWER, ESQ.

45. THE VIRGIN AND CHILD AND ANGELS.

The Virgin, in white and blue robes, the Spanish colours for her dress, stands facing within an apse, and holds the Infant Child to her breast ; on either side kneels an angel, one playing on a lute, the other on a harp. Panel, 18 × 13½ in.
This picture, which dates from about 1480-1490, was acquired at Salamanca, and was probably painted in that city. The architectural background represents the apse of the Seo Viéjo, or old cathedral at Salamanca.

By an EARLY FLEMISH MASTER WORKING IN SPAIN.

Lent by SIR CHARLES ROBINSON.

46. PORTRAIT OF A LADY.

Half-length figure slightly turned to left, her hands folded, dark dress with white sleeves, and white and gold yoke ; yellow head-dress embroidered with jewels. Panel, 8 × 6¼ in.

By CORNELIUS DE LYONS. Lent by GEORGE SALTING, ESQ.

47. ENGELBERT, COUNT OF NASSAU AND GOVERNOR OF BRABANT (d. 1504).

A staunch adherent of the Burgundian dynasty, he was taken prisoner at the Battle of Nancy, where Charles the Bold perished ; subsequently distinguished himself in the Battle of Guinegate ; died in 1504, and was interred at Breda, where there is a magnificent monument to him and his wife, a Princess of Baden.
Small half-length figure to left, in black dress and cap, and wearing the Collar of the Golden Fleece ; on his left hand is perched a hooded falcon ; his right resting on the frame of the picture, which is inscribed in Lombardic characters, "Engelbert, Count de Nassau," and dated above 1497. Panel, 13 × 9½ in.

EARLY FLEMISH SCHOOL. Lent by WICKHAM FLOWER, ESQ.

C

48. THE VIRGIN AND CHILD.

In a Flemish interior the Virgin sits on a bench with the Child on her lap, and about to give Him the breast. She wears a white robe, while the dark blue sleeves of her dress show at the wrists. The Child is naked, but lies on a white cloth. The Virgin's head is relieved against a wickerwork roundel, which acts both as a fire-screen and a halo. Her left elbow rests on a piece of furniture, in which is a chalice. In the left of the bench is an open book on a red cushion. In the background an open window affords a glimpse over the market-place of a town. Panel, 26 × 20¾ in.

By the "MAITRE DE FLEMALLE."   Lent by M. LÉON DE SOMZÉE.

49. CHRIST AND THE WOMAN OF CANAAN.

Outside the walls of a city in a landscape with buildings and hills : Christ in the centre in a blue robe, His right hand raised, is listening to the earnest appeal of the Woman of Canaan, who kneels behind Him, her hands clasped in supplication : behind her are her two attendants, one of whom is addressing St. Peter ; before our Lord are two other disciples. Panel, 31 × 22 in.
This picture has formerly been identified as a " Noli Me tangere."

By HERRI DE BLES (CIVETTA).   Lent by CHARLES BUTLER, ESQ.

50. ST. LEONARD RELEASING THE CAPTIVES.

Full-length figure of the Saint, in black habit of the Benedictine Order, holding book in left hand, and with his right liberating a captive, who issues from a prison on the left ; another captive is seen at a window ; soldiers are falling from the roof ; landscape background and golden sky. Panel, 60 × 27½ in.
EARLY FLEMISH SCHOOL.   Lent by LADY TREVELYAN.

51. ST. VICTOR WITH THE DONOR.

Three-quarter length figure of the Saint to left in armour and red mantle ; in his right hand he holds his banner and shield ; his left rests on the shoulder of the donor, who in ecclesiastical robes kneels at his side in prayer ; distant landscape. Panel, 22 × 18¼ in.
By HUGO VAN DER GOES.   Lent by the CORPORATION OF THE CITY OF GLASGOW.

52. ST. ANNE WITH THE VIRGIN AND CHILD, AND ST. BERNARD AND ST. ANTHONY OF PADUA. An Altar-piece.

In the centre panel St. Anne seated on a throne and holding on her right knee the Virgin, who is supporting the Child ; He turns the leaves of a book held by St. Anne ; she wears a purple robe, long red mantle and white head-dress ; the Virgin is in a lilac dress with a blue mantle ; on the base of the throne is a rich Eastern carpet ; on the left panel stands St. Bernard in embroidered red chasuble, and wearing a jewelled mitre ; his right hand is in the act of benediction, and in the left he holds the pastoral staff ; on the right panel is St. Anthony of Padua in his friar's habit, the cross in his right hand, and on his left an open book on which the Child is seated ; in the background of the panels are landscapes with a church and a castle. Panel, centre, 94 × 38 in. ; sides, 94 × 28 in.
From the Collection of Cardinal Antonio Despuyg de Palma.

By GHEERAERT DAVID.   Lent by M. LÉON DE SOMZÉE.

53. ST. LEONARD CONDUCTING CAPTIVES TO A MONASTERY.

Full-length figures : the Saint habited as in No. 50, conducting three captives to his monastery, at the doorway of which are other monks, waiting to receive them : landscape background and golden sky.   Panel, 60 × 27½ in.

EARLY FLEMISH SCHOOL.   Lent by LADY TREVELYAN.

54. THE VIRGIN AND CHILD ENTHRONED, AND ANGELS.

Full-length figure of the Virgin, seated on a throne and holding the Child upon her lap ; He stretches out His right hand to take a flower from an angel, who leans on the left of the throne ; another angel on the right is reading a scroll ; the throne is covered with an Eastern carpet.   Panel, 27 × 20½ in.

By HANS MEMLINC.   Lent by MRS. STEPHENSON CLARKE.

55. THE CALL OF ST. MATTHEW.

On the left our Lord in grey, facing the spectator is turning to the right and addressing St. Matthew, who is bending forward across the counter of his office, holding in his left hand a hat with brown scarf ; on the counter are a coffer, a dish containing coins, a money-box, an inkstand and a pen, and some account-books, one of which is open and shows entries ; on the left outside the office are St. Peter and two other Apostles, and in the background two towers with a mountain in the distance ; on the right are files of papers, and in the middle a tablet with scriptural references suspended by a ring.   Panel, 27 × 33¾ in.   See *Catalogue of the Northbrook Collection,* No 26.

By JAN VAN HEMESSEN.   Lent by the EARL OF NORTHBROOK, K.C.I.E.

56. THE VIRGIN AND CHILD.

Half-length figure of the Virgin seated facing, holding the Child in her arms ; His lower limbs are wrapped in a white cloth ; she wears blue dress and red cloak, and her head is bound with a black band ; on the left are a hunting scene and a pond with swans and buildings ; on the right, a man coming down a road in a wood, and water gushing from rocks ; in the centre background buildings and distant landscape. Panel, 25½ × 19½ in.

EARLY FLEMISH SCHOOL.   Lent by LADY TREVELYAN.

57. PHILIP LE BON, DUKE OF BURGUNDY (1396–1467) AND HIS THIRD WIFE, ISABELLA OF PORTUGAL (1397–1472).   A Diptych. (See No. 59.)

On the left panel half-length figure of Philip to right, wearing black cloak and black hat with jewel, around his neck the Order of the Golden Fleece ; his right hand is shown.   On the right panel half-length figure of Isabella to left in low-cut crimson velvet dress trimmed with ermine, and gold embroidered bodice, massive gold chain around her neck ; high gold embroidered head-dress with veil ; her left hand is shown.   Panel (oval top), each 6½ × 4¾ in.   From the Magniac Collection.

EARLY FLEMISH SCHOOL.   Lent by WICKHAM FLOWER, ESQ.

58. THE ENTOMBMENT. Part of a Triptych.

In the foreground Christ is being laid in the tomb ; St. Mary Magdalene kneels in front, and around are grouped the Virgin, St. John, the holy women, and Joseph of Arimathea : wooded and rocky background, through which flows a river ; a castle on the right ; on the reverse is a figure of the Virgin, part of an *Annunciation*. Panel, 12½ × 5 in.

By HANS MEMLINC.   Lent by SIR HENRY THOMPSON, BART.

59. PHILIP LE BON, DUKE OF BURGUNDY (1396–1467).

Son of Jean "Sans-peur" and Margaret of Bavaria, succeeded to the Duchy of Burgundy on the assassination of his father, supported the cause in France of Henry V. of England, but afterwards allied himself to Charles VII., and assisted in the expulsion of the English from France. He instituted the Order of the Golden Fleece in honour of his third wife, Isabella of Portugal (see No. 57). He died at Bruges, 15th July, 1467.
Small half-length figure to right ; hands folded, and holding paper ; black dress and cap with jewel ; around his neck the Order of the Golden Fleece. Panel, 12½ × 8½ in

By ROGIER VAN DER WEYDEN.   Lent by GEORGE SALTING, ESQ.

60. CHARLES V., THE EMPEROR (1516–1558).

The Emperor in rich armour and plumed helmet, on a white charger, advancing to the left, an arrow in his right hand and the reins of his horse in his left ; before him on the ground lies a Moorish king clutching at a sceptre with his left hand, and raising his right as if to implore the conqueror's mercy ; this group is within an archway ; in the background a stone wall, on which grows a shrub. Panel, 14¾ × 11½ in.
Formerly attributed to Albert Dürer. See *Catalogue of the Northbrook Collection*, No. 27.

By BERNARD VAN ORLEY.   Lent by the EARL OF NORTHBROOK, K.C.I.E.

61. THE VIRGIN AND CHILD ENTHRONED.

The Virgin in blue dress, seated facing, within a richly carved throne ; she supports on her knees the Child, Who looks down at a winged cherub standing on the footpiece of the throne, offering Him some flowers ; in front of the cherub is another playing on the clarionet ; opposite are four others playing and singing from a book ; through the pillars of the throne on the left are seen an ox and an angel kneeling before the Virgin, who stands in the doorway of a house ; through the pillars on the right is a garden, in which are Joseph, holding a staff and a lighted candle, and farther off an angel and a swan ; beyond are buildings. Panel, 13½ × 9¾ in.
See *Catalogue of the Northbrook Collection*, No. 20.

By JAN GOSSAERT, called MABUSE.   Lent by the EARL OF NORTHBROOK, K.C.I.E.

62. THE VIRGIN AND CHILD.

Under an arch small half-length figure of the Virgin, facing, supporting the Child with both hands ; He holds a flower in His left hand, and grasps with His right the white cloth on which He reclines ; the Virgin wears blue robe, red mantle, and white head-dress, her head bound with jewelled band ; on a parapet in front is displayed an oriental carpet ; landscape background.   Panel, 15 × 11¼ in.

By DIERICK BOUTS.   Lent by the EARL OF NORTHBROOK, K.C.I.E.

63. THE VIRGIN AND CHILD.

The Virgin in a pensive attitude, seated within a stone alcove, holds the Child with her right arm, and rests her left on the ledge of the seat. The Child is caressing His mother's chin with His right hand, and has His left arm around her neck. She wears crimson dress, lilac mantle, which she holds with her left hand, and a green kerchief across the shoulders. The Child's lower limbs are wrapped in transparent muslin. The floor is a rich tessellated pavement.   Panel, 22⅞ × 16½ in.

This picture, formerly ascribed to Hans Memlinc and to Jan Gossaert (Mabuse), is probably by the Master of the Mater Dolorosa in the Church of Notre Dame at Bruges. See *Catalogue of the Northbrook Collection*, No. 4.

EARLY FLEMISH SCHOOL.   Lent by the EARL OF NORTHBROOK, K.C.I.E.

64. ECCE HOMO.

In the foreground Christ is seen taking leave of His mother, who has fallen back supported by one of the Marys, near whom stands another, whilst Mary Magdalene kneels on the extreme left ; on the right are St. Peter, St John and two other Apostles ; in the middle distance stands Pilate on a raised terrace and holding a thorny wand he shows to the people Christ crowned with thorns and clad in a white mantle, which two men hold up exposing to view His body torn with stripes ; below are the shouting populace ; on the wall of Pilate's house are the words *Ecce Homo* ; in the background, buildings of a town and numerous figures, rocks and dark clouds. Panel, 17½ × 13 in.

This picture has been ascribed to Cornelius Engelbrechsten and to Lucas van Leyden. The background is almost exactly like an engraving by Lucas van Leyden, entitled, "Ecce Homo," *Bartsch*, viii. 378, No. 71 ; reproduced in the *Berlin Reproductions*. Vol. i., No. 18. The figures in the foreground are different.   See *Catalogue of the Northbrook Collection*, No. 6.

EARLY FLEMISH SCHOOL.   Lent by the EARL OF NORTHBROOK, K.C.I.E.

65. THE VIRGIN AND CHILD.

Small full-length figure of the Virgin seated on a low wall, holding the Child upon her lap ; with her right hand she plucks a flower, which grows on the wall beside her ; behind her a cloth of estate ; distant landscape in the background.   Panel, 10½ × 8½ in.

By HUGO VAN DER GOES.   Lent by MRS. STEPHENSON CLARKE.

66. SAINTS CECILIA, MARGARET, AGATHA AND DOROTHY.

The Saints are seated in a garden enclosed by a trellis-worked fence ; beyond which are four houses ; the background is occupied by hills, with two castles in the distance ; in the garden are a peacock, a peahen, and two parroquets. St. Cecilia, in lilac dress, has an organ in her left hand, and a falcon on her right. St. Margaret, in crimson dress, holds two white pinks, and is raising her right hand to make the sign of the cross over the dragon which lies at her feet. St. Agatha, in scarlet dress, holds up a pair of pincers with her breast. St Dorothy, in violet, has a sword in her right hand and a flower in her left hand. Two panels (in one frame), $13\frac{1}{4} \times 8\frac{3}{4}$ in. Ascribed to Hans Memlinc and to Gerard van der Meire. From the De Merckem Collection. See *Catalogue of the Northbrook Collection*, No. 3.

EARLY FLEMISH SCHOOL.   Lent by the EARL OF NORTHBROOK, K.C.I.E.

67. THE VIRGIN AND CHILD, WITH DONORS.

The Virgin seated on a raised daïs under a canopy, covered with a cloth of estate, offers her breast to the Child, Whom she supports with her left hand ; she wears blue dress and red mantle, and white head-dress ; the Child is seated on a white cloth ; on either side kneel the donor and his wife, behind whom are their children ; in the background a high stone wall, on which are peacocks and peahen, and in the distance trees ; the respective ages of the donor, his wife, and two of his children are painted on the wall. Panel, 26×25 in.

By JAN MOSTERT.   Lent by the EARL OF NORTHBROOK, K.C.I.E.

68. THE VISION OF ST. ILDEPHONSUS.

The Virgin appearing to St. Ildephonsus, Bishop of Toledo, after his refutation of the heresy of Helvidius. The Saint kneels before an altar in a large church ; he is looking up with outstretched hands at the Virgin, who appears on the left accompanied by three angels, and is about to vest him with a red chasuble ; behind the Saint on the right kneel three monks, one holding an open book, the second looking up at the vision, and the third absorbed in prayer ; in the background a procession of monks chanting. Panel, $15\frac{3}{4} \times 13\frac{1}{2}$ in. See *Catalogue of the Northbrook Collection*, No. 5.

EARLY FLEMISH SCHOOL.   Lent by the EARL OF NORTHBROOK, K.C.I.E.

69. THE VIRGIN AND CHILD.

Three-quarter length figure of the Virgin seated under a canopy, wearing dark blue dress and crimson mantle ; hair long and falling over her shoulders ; a jewel, fastened to a band, above her forehead. She supports with her right hand the Infant Saviour, Who, seated on a linen cloth in her lap, takes from His mother a nosegay of red and white pinks, and with His right caresses a parroquet. Panel, $10\frac{3}{4} \times 7\frac{1}{2}$ in. This panel is attributed to the year 1457. See *Catalogue of the Northbrook Collection*, No. 25.

By JAN VAN EYCK.   Lent by the EARL OF NORTHBROOK, K.C.I.E.

70. ECCE HOMO.

Christ crowned with thorns seated within a building, His hands joined and His feet crossed, white raiment over His knees ; in the background are three figures. Signed, JOHANNES MALBODIVS INVENIT, and dated 1527. Panel, 9¼ × 7½ in.

By JAN GOSSAERT, called MABUSE.   Lent by ISAAC FALCKE, ESQ.

71. THE VIRGIN AND CHILD.

Half-length figure of the Virgin, facing before a wall on which are plants, supporting in her arms, on a white cloth, the Child, Who is feeding at her breast ; she wears a blue robe with gold embroidered sleeves, and white head-dress with jewel in centre. Panel, 20 × 15 in. From the Ruston Collection.

By JAN GOSSAERT, called MABUSE.   Lent by the EARL OF NORTHBROOK, K.C.I.E.

72. THE VIRGIN AND CHILD.

Three-quarter length figure of the Virgin in blue dress, pale blue embroidered mantle and fine cambric veil ; she supports with her right hand the Infant on a white cloth, and holds with her left a book, the leaves of which He is turning ; on the left stands a carved wooden aumbrye, with a latten candlestick on it ; green curtain background. Panel, 14½ × 9¾ in.

From the Weyer and Heath Collections. See *Catalogue of the Northbrook Collection* No. 8.

EARLY FLEMISH SCHOOL.   Lent by the EARL OF NORTHBROOK, K.C.I.E.

73. ST. JOHN IN PATMOS.

Small full-length figure of the Saint, facing, hands clasped, standing in a landscape ; scarlet robe ; in the background a stag feeding, and buildings by the sea. Panel, 10 × 4½ in.

BY JOACHIM PATINIR.   Lent by MARTIN COLNAGHI, ESQ.

74. ST. MARY MAGDALENE READING.

Small half-length figure of the Magdalene to left in red and black dress, holding an illuminated missal in her hands ; on a table in front of her is a small vase ; around her head is the nimbus. Panel, 17½ × 14 in.

By JAN MOSTERT.   Lent by CHARLES BUTLER, ESQ.

75. THE HOLY FAMILY.

The Virgin, in red and blue drapery, is seated beside a table with a green cover, and supports the Child in her arms ; He is clothed in a transparent garment, and leaning forward plays with a rosary strung over His shoulders ; on the table is a covered glass goblet of wine, a folded napkin, a cut orange and a knife ; on the left St. Joseph, in a large straw hat, is reading a roll of manuscript ; landscape on the left. Panel, 28¼ × 21 in. For similar treatment of this subject see No. 43.

By THE MASTER OF " THE DEATH OF THE VIRGIN " (in the Munich Gallery)
Lent by CAPTAIN G. L. HOLFORD, C.I.E.

76. THE VIRGIN AND CHILD AND ST. JOSEPH.

Three-quarter length figure of the Virgin seated to right on a throne, and holding the Child to her breast ; she wears blue dress and red mantle ; above, cherubim support-ing a canopy ; on the right is seen St. Joseph gathering palm-fruit ; and in the back-ground, landscape with buildings. Panel, 35 × 26½ in. Exhibited at Manchester in 1857, and at Leeds in 1868. From the Roscoe Collection. Waagen iii, p. 236.

By BERNARD VAN ORLEY.

Lent by the TRUSTEES OF THE ROYAL INSTITUTION, LIVERPOOL.

77. THE VIRGIN AND CHILD.

Small full-length figures ; the Virgin, in blue dress and red mantle over her knees, and white head-dress, seated facing under a tree and holding the Child on her knees ; their right hands support a small globe, and in His left is a crown ; two angels above hold a crown over the Virgin's head ; in the background, buildings and hills with trees ; the Salutation is seen on the left, and the Annunciation on the right. Panel, 12½ × 9½ in. From the Roscoe Collection.

EARLY FLEMISH SCHOOL.

Lent by the TRUSTEES OF THE ROYAL INSTITUTION, LIVERPOOL.

78. MOSES AND THE BURNING BUSH AND GIDEON AND THE FLEECE.

Two volets of an altar-piece, joined to form a single panel ; on the left Moses kneeling before the Burning Bush, above which appears the Creator ; on the right kneels Gideon, the Fleece on the ground at his side ; above is an Angel ; in the background, city and landscape. Panel, 29 × 15½ in.

By DIERICK BOUTS.   Lent by CHARLES T. D. CREWS, ESQ.

79. TWO OLD MUSICIANS.

An old man and a woman seated in a landscape ; the man is playing a lute, and the woman a violin. Panel, 4¼ × 3½ in.

By LUCAS VAN LEYDEN.   Lent by J. FLETCHER MOULTON, ESQ., Q.C., M.P.

80. THE VIRGIN AND CHILD.

Small full-length figure of the Virgin enthroned under an elaborately carved canopy, holding the Child on her lap ; buildings and landscape in the background. Panel, 11½ × 7¾ in. (circular top).

By JAN MOSTERT.   Lent by CHARLES BUTLER, ESQ.

81. CHRIST APPEARING TO HIS DISCIPLES AFTER HIS RESURRECTION.

In the foreground on the right Christ stands on the shore of the Sea of Tiberias, and holds up His right hand with a gesture of command to St. Peter, who has thrown himself from his boat, and with clasped hands runs eagerly through the shallow water to the bank ; the two central figures are separated by a tall acacia tree ; in the boat which the Saint has quitted are the sons of Zebedee drawing in a net ; in the middle distance is another boat with three other disciples similarly engaged, and beyond a rocky shore with many buildings ; on the right is a group of Christ and the disciples taking food round a fire, and behind them a hill with a city.   Panel, 12 × 18 in. (See St. John, xxi.)

By JOACHIM PATINIR.   Lent by Sir KENNETH MUIR MACKENZIE, K.C.B.

82.   THE VIRGIN AND CHILD.

Full-length figure of the Virgin seated facing, under a canopy ; she holds the Infant on her knees, and gives Him a flower with her left hand ; He is seated on a white cloth and holds a parroquet with his right ; on a ledge in front are cherries, a cut lemon, and a knife ; architectural frame and windows in the background.   Panel, 31½ × 24½ in.

By JAN VAN EYCK.   Lent by J. FLETCHER MOULTON, ESQ., Q.C., M.P.

83.   THE DEPOSITION.

At the foot of the Cross lies the dead body of the Christ, His head supported by St. John ; at His feet kneels the Virgin, who is kissing His right hand ; at her side Mary Magdalene, who supports her head with her left hand, and places her right on her shoulder ; on the extreme left kneels the female donor, praying ; blue landscape in the distance.   Panel, 19½ × 18¼ in.

By LUCAS VAN LEYDEN.   Lent by RALPH BROCKLEBANK, Esq.

84.   ADAM AND EVE.

Two full-length, life-size, nude figures ; Adam on the left, leaning against a tree, the forefinger of his right hand is held to his lips ; his left arm is around Eve's shoulders; her right hand is placed on his left shoulder ; in her left hand is the stalk with the fruit ; above them on a branch is a serpent, his head thrust between theirs ; in the distance landscape with fountain.   Panel, 65 × 43 in.

This picture has been in the Royal Collection since the time of Henry VIII. ; but it was temporarily disposed of during the Commonwealth.

By JAN GOSSAERT, called MABUSE.

Lent by HER MAJESTY THE QUEEN (HAMPTON COURT).

85.   THE VIRGIN AND CHILD IN A GARDEN.

The Virgin, seated facing on a bench with tall upright back covered with a cloth of estate, holds the Child on her knee with her right hand, and with her left supports a book, the leaves of which He is turning ; the Virgin wears a flowing scarlet robe with a border of gold and jewels ; a fillet confines her hair, and is fastened by a jewel on the forehead ; in the foreground is a mass of flowers, amongst which is laid a cushion of white and gold brocade, on which the Virgin's feet are supported ; on the right and left is a landscape with water-mill and distant castle.   Panel, 35½ × 30¼ in.

Several repetitions of this "Virgin and Child" exist, but with different backgrounds. The monogram of Albert Dürer with the date 1513 on the left is a forgery.

SCHOOL OF GHEERAERT DAVID.   Lent by the EARL OF CRAWFORD, K.T.

86. THE JUDGMENT OF SOLOMON.

In the centre on a throne is seated Solomon, his sceptre in his right hand ; before him are the two women, one kneeling, and between them on the base of the throne lies the dead child ; on the left is a soldier drawing his sword about to divide the living child ; around the throne are grouped attendants ; in the foreground a small dog, his front feet resting on a bone. Panel (arched top), 22¼ × 15¾ in. From the Howard Galton Collection.

By LUCAS VAN LEYDEN.   Lent by SIR WILLIAM FARRER.

87. CHRIST AND ST. JOHN EMBRACING.

Christ and St. John, as children, seated on a black velvet cushion under a highly decorative portico, and embracing ; above,¡a red canopy ; through the portico is seen a landscape. Panel, 28¼ × 21¼ in.

By BERNARD VAN ORLEY.   Lent by RALPH BROCKLEBANK, ESQ.

88. THE ANNUNCIATION.

On the right seated on the floor beside a canopied bed draped with scarlet the Virgin reads from an illuminated book upon her knee ; the Archangel enters on the left and advances towards her carrying in his hands a golden sceptre ; above them hovers the holy dove ; on the tiled floor in the background are a lily in a blue and white porcelain pot, and a seat with a scarlet cushion. Panel, circular, 8 in.

EARLY FLEMISH SCHOOL.   Lent by SIR KENNETH MUIR MACKENZIE, K.C.B.

89. PORTRAIT OF A LADY.

Small bust to left, in black dress, lace ruff and cap ; a rustic scene in the background, with two men engaged in a duel. Panel, 10¼ × 8½ in. From the Gibson-Craig Collection.

EARLY FLEMISH SCHOOL.   Lent by RALPH BROCKLEBANK, ESQ.

90. HEADS OF JEWS AND A SOLDIER.

Heads, facing, of a crowd of Jews and a soldier ; all shouting, some gesticulating. Panel, 8¾ × 23 in. From the W. Graham Collection.
Probably a fragment of an "Ecce Homo," and representing a portion of the crowd.

By QUINTEN MATSYS.   Lent by RALPH BROCKLEBANK, ESQ.

91. PORTRAIT OF A YOUNG NOBLEMAN, AND THE CONVERSION OF ST. HUBERT.

Three-quarter length figure seated to left, his hands gloved and joined ; in red velvet tunic and brown fur lined coat and black cap ; on the left is depicted a scene representing the conversion of St. Hubert ; city on wooded hill in the background. Panel, 37½ × 29 in. Exhibited at Manchester in 1857 and at Leeds in 1868. From the Roscoe Collection. Waagen, iii., p. 236.

By LUCAS VAN LEYDEN.

Lent by the TRUSTEES OF THE ROYAL INSTITUTION, LIVERPOOL.

92. THE ADORATION OF THE MAGI AND ST. HUBERT AND ST. JAMES OF COMPOSTELLA. A Triptych.

In the centre panel is represented the Adoration of the Magi ; on the right volet is St. Hubert holding his bow and arrows, and on the left volet St. James of Compostella leaning on his staff. Panel, centre, 10¾ × 7½ in. ; sides, 10¾ × 3 in.

By JAN MOSTERT. Lent by MESSRS. P. AND D. COLNAGHI AND CO.

93. THE MADONNA PRAYING.

Small half-length figure of the Virgin to left, her hands folded in prayer ; pink under-dress, blue mantle, and white drapery over her head. Panel, 14½ × 11½ in.

By JUSTUS VAN CLEEF. Lent by the TRUSTEES OF THE BOWES MUSEUM.

94. THE VIRGIN AND CHILD.

Interior of a chamber, with a bed on the left ; the Virgin seated feeding the Child at her breast, Whom she supports with her right arm ; she wears blue dress and crimson mantle. Panel, 24 × 18 in. Exhibited at Manchester, 1857. From the Fuller-Russell Collection.

By QUINTEN MATSYS. Lent by WICKHAM FLOWER, ESQ.

95. FILIBERTA OF SAVOY, WIFE OF GIULIANO II. DE' MEDICI, DUKE OF NEMOURS (1498–1524.)

Bust slightly turned to right, looking at the spectator ; hands crossed ; blue dress and brown cloak ; white head-dress. Panel, 19½ × 13½ in.
On the back of the panel is the stamp of Cardinal Sigismondo de' Medici.

EARLY FLEMISH SCHOOL. Lent by HUGH P. LANE, ESQ.

96. ADORATION OF THE MAGI.

The Virgin seated on the left with the Child in her lap ; in front of them kneels an aged wise man in adoration ; behind are grouped two other magi, holding rich gold vessels, and numerous figures in attitudes expressive of praise and worship ; on a ledge in front, a sceptre and a gold vase, with cover ; in the distance are seen some blue mountains ; half-length figures. Panel, 39 × 30½ in.

By QUINTEN MATSYS. Lent by H. R. HUGHES OF KINMEL, ESQ.

97. MARY TUDOR, DUCHESS OF SUFFOLK (1498–1583). See No. 30.

Half-length figure to the left, in black dress, with ermine sleeves and fur collar ; black cap ; round her neck black ribbon with pendant jewel ; jewelled waistband ; she holds in her right hand a folded letter. Panel, $21\frac{1}{2} \times 16\frac{1}{2}$ in.

By JAN GOSSAERT, called MABUSE.   Lent by the EARL BROWNLOW.

98. PORTRAIT OF A MAN.

Small half-length figure turned to left, his left hand resting on a ledge before him ; black dress edged with fur, white shirt and black cap. Panel, $12\frac{1}{2} \times 10$ in.

EARLY FLEMISH SCHOOL.

99. TWELVE SCENES OF THE PASSION.   (In Central Hall.)

(1) The Last Supper ; (2) The Agony in the Garden ; (3) The Betrayal ; (4) Ecce Homo ; (5) Our Lord mocked ; (6) The Scourging ; (7) The Crowning with thorns ; (8) St. Veronica presenting the Veil ; (9) The Crucifixion ; (10) The Entombment ; (11) The Descent into Hades ; (12) The Resurrection. Panel, $6\frac{1}{2} \times 3\frac{1}{2}$ in.

By ROGIER VAN DER WEYDEN.   Lent by J. FLETCHER MOULTON, ESQ., Q.C., M.P.

NORTH ROOM.

WORKS OF SIR PETER PAUL RUBENS, ETC.

PETER PAUL RUBENS was born at Siegen, in Westphalia, 28th June, 1577, on the feast of St. Peter and St. Paul. His father, Jan Rubens, was an alderman of Antwerp, but, on account of religious troubles, he removed with his family to Cologne. On the death of her husband, in 1587, Rubens's mother, with her children, returned to Antwerp. Here Rubens studied under Tobias Verhaagt, Adam van Noort, and Otto van Veen, the latter being the most celebrated painter of his time at Antwerp. In 1600 Rubens went to Italy and entered the service of Vincenzio Gonzaga, Duke of Mantua, and in 1605 was sent on a mission by the Duke to Philip III. of Spain, and whilst at Madrid he painted several portraits of the Spanish nobility. Rubens returned to Antwerp in 1608, where he was induced to remain by the Archduke Albert, then Governor of the Netherlands, and he was appointed court-painter to Albert and Isabella in 1609. At the invitation of Marie de' Medici Rubens visited Paris in 1620, and there received the commission for his celebrated series of pictures for the new palace of the Luxembourg, commemorating the marriage of the princess with Henry IV. of France. In 1628 Rubens was sent by the Infanta Isabella, widow of the Archduke Albert, on a diplomatic mission to Philip IV. of Spain, and in the following year he came on a similar mission to Charles I. of England, by whom he was knighted in 1630. On his return to the Netherlands he settled at Antwerp, and later on at the Chateau de Steen near Mechlin. His death took place on the 30th May, 1640, and he was in the first place interred in the vault of the Fourment family ; but two years afterwards the body was removed to a special chapel built out from the church of St. Jacques at Antwerp. His last work was the altar-piece for the church of St. Peter at Cologne, on which he expended an amount of care unusual with him.

103. SIR PETER PAUL RUBENS (1577–1640).

Small half-length figure in chiaroscuro ; slightly turned to left, and looking at the spectator ; his left arm rests on a ledge ; with right hand he raises his cloak. Panel, 9½ × 7½ in.

By SIR ANTHONY VAN DYCK.   Lent by G. E. MARTIN, ESQ.

104. PORTRAIT OF A LADY.

Small half-length front, head turned to right ; yellow dress with jewel ; pearl neck-lace : long brown hair. Panel, 9 × 7½ in.

By GONZALES COQUES.   Lent by HUGH P. LANE, ESQ.

105. DANIEL IN THE DEN OF LIONS.

Finished sketch for the large picture (see No. 145).   Panel 18 × 25½ in.

By RUBENS.   Lent by SIR WILLIAM FARRER.

106. PRINCESS ELIZABETH, DAUGHTER OF JAMES I. (1596–1662).

Married in 1613 Frederick, Elector Palatine, became for a short time Queen of Bohemia, and after a life of many vicissitudes died in London in 1662.
Youthful three-quarter length figure turned slightly to right, looking at the spectator ; red gold-embroidered dress, lace ruffs and cuffs ; coronet of pearls with aigrette on her head and jewel above her forehead ; around her neck a chain with jewel pendant and pearl ; earrings of pearls.   Panel (oval), 25 × 19½ in.

Lent by GEORGE JOHNSTONE, ESQ., M.D.

107. THE HOLY FAMILY.

Three-quarter length figures ; the Virgin, in red dress and blue mantle, holding the Infant Jesus, Who is seated on a white cushion on her lap ; she is looking down lovingly at an angel who is presenting a basket of fruit to the Child ; on the right is St. Joseph looking on ; behind the figures is a stone wall and a red curtain ; on the left a landscape with trees, the clouds illumined by the evening light.   Canvas, 47 × 64 in.

By RUBENS.   Lent by CHARLES MORRISON, ESQ.

108. ROME TRIUMPHANT.   A Sketch.

Rome, seated on a throne beneath a canopy, is crowned by Victory ; near her stands a man holding a standard ; on the right is a warrior, a man holding a horse and other figures ; on the left are captives and a trophy ; before the throne are the wolf and twins, bound captives, and two eagles.   Panel, 19½ × 25 in.   From the Calonne Collection.   (Buchanan's *Memoirs*, i., p. 244.)

By RUBENS.   Lent by SIR FRANCIS COOK, BART.

109. NICOLAS ROCKOX.

Burgomaster of Antwerp and an intimate friend of Rubens.
Bust, life-size, to left ; black coat, white ruff.   Panel, 24 × 19 in.

By RUBENS.   Lent by SIR FRANCIS COOK, BART.

110. THE FLIGHT INTO EGYPT.

Small full-length figures ; the Virgin, with the Infant Saviour in her arms, is mounted on an ass which is led by an angel ; another angel soars over their heads, bearing a lighted torch ; St. Joseph follows behind ; other angels are seen above ; the moon shines through the trees of a wood through which they are passing.   Panel, 19 × 25 in.

By RUBENS.   Lent by the EARL BROWNLOW.

111. THETIS PLUNGING ACHILLES INTO THE RIVER STYX. A Sketch.

The nymph, clothed in thin raiment round her loins, stands on the bank of the
stream and immerses the infant into its mystic waters ; Destiny, bearing a blazing
torch in her hand and with the distaff stuck in her girdle, stands at her side, viewing
the ceremony ; on each side are *termini* of Pluto and Proserpine, supporting a
cornice decorated with festoons ; in the background, the Styx with boats and rocks.
Panel, 15 × 12½ in.

This picture and Nos. 112—116 illustrating, in succession, the life and actions of
Achilles, were painted by the artist for his royal patron, Charles I., as models to be
worked into tapestry. Engraved by Ertinger (1679) and by B. Baron (1724). Smith,
Cat. Rais., ii. p. 250. Exhibited at Manchester, 1857.

BY RUBENS.   Lent by the Right Hon. A. H. SMITH-BARRY.

112. THE INSTRUCTION OF ACHILLES. A Sketch.

Achilles is mounted on the back of the centaur Cheiron, who, while he teaches him the
art of riding, is also inculcating other lessons of useful knowledge ; landscape background ; the *termini* at the sides represent Apollo and Æsculapius, who support a
cornice adorned with flowers. Panel, 15 × 12½ in. Smith, *Cat. Rais.*, ii. p. 251.
See No. 111. Exhibited at Manchester, 1857.

By RUBENS.   Lent by the Right Hon. A. H. SMITH-BARRY.

113. THETIS RECEIVING ARMS FROM VULCAN FOR ACHILLES. A Sketch.

Thetis, accompanied by Cupid and a nymph, is stepping out of the sea and receives a
shield from the hands of Vulcan ; a Cyclops is seen bringing forward a cuirass in his
arms, and a Cupid is bearing off a helmet to a Triton ; the tools of Vulcan lie in the
foreground ; the *termini* at the sides represent Jupiter and Juno, supporting a cornice
ornamented with festoons of fruit and two Cupids. Panel, 15 × 17½ in. Smith,
Cat. Rais., ii. p. 252. See No. 111. Exhibited at Manchester, 1857.

By RUBENS.   Lent by the Right Hon. A. H. SMITH-BARRY.

114. ACHILLES VANQUISHING HECTOR. A Sketch.

The hero, clad in the armour made for him by Vulcan, is represented fighting with
Hector, whom he has pierced in the neck with his spear ; the Trojan chief sinks on his
hand and knee to the ground ; Achilles is accompanied by Pallas ; the walls of
Troy, with numerous warriors on the battlements, and the flying enemy, appear in the
distance ; at the sides are *termini* of Mars and Hercules, supporting a cornice enriched
with festoons of fruit and two Cupids. Panel, 15 × 15½ in. Smith, *Cat. Rais.*,
ii. p. 252. See No. 111. Exhibited at Manchester, 1857.

By RUBENS.   Lent by the Right Hon. A. H. SMITH-BARRY.

115. THE ANGER OF ACHILLES AGAINST AGAMEMNON. A Sketch.

Achilles, in anger, stands on the right, and is in the act of drawing his sword to revenge the loss of his captive, Briseïs ; but is prevented by Pallas, who cautions him to forbear ; Agamemnon, also enraged, is attempting to rise from his throne to encounter the hero, but is restrained by Nestor ; other Greeks are present ; the *termini* at the sides represent Envy and Passion, who support a cornice decorated with festoons of fruit and Cupids.   Panel, 15 × 13¾ in.   Smith, *Cat. Rais.*, ii. p. 351. See No. 111.   Exhibited at Manchester, 1857.

By RUBENS.   Lent by the Right Hon. A. H. SMITH-BARRY.

116. THE DEATH OF ACHILLES. A Sketch.

The hero, wounded in the heel by an arrow from the bow of Paris, is sinking at the side of the altar at which he was espousing Polyxena ; he is supported by one of his attendants, who, as well as the high priest and a second attendant at the altar, are in an attitude of alarm ; Paris, accompanied by Apollo, is seen at the entrance of the temple ; in front a fox devouring an eagle, emblematic of cunning overcoming valour; at the sides are *termini* of Venus and Apollo, supporting a cornice decorated with festoons of fruit and two Cupids.   Panel, 15 × 15½.   Smith, *Cat. Rais.*, p. 253.   See No. 111.   Exhibited at Manchester, 1857.

By RUBENS.   Lent by the Right Hon. A. H. SMITH-BARRY.

117. THE WILD BOAR HUNT.

Landscape ; in the foreground on the right are men on horseback and dogs pursuing a wild boar, which rushes towards a man holding a spear, who stands behind a fallen dead tree ; two other figures with spears stand on either side of the tree ; on the left is a man blowing a horn, and another holding a dog ; further in the background are seen youths and dogs pursuing another boar.   Canvas, 62½ × 80 in.

By RUBENS.   Lent by SIR CHARLES ROBINSON.

118. THE WILD BOAR HUNT. A Sketch.

To left of the composition, Diana, having discharged her arrow at the boar, is leaping over a fallen tree, surrounded by her dogs ; in the centre is the boar brought to bay, whilst on the right a man attacks it with a spear ; in the background are horsemen and a nymph blowing a horn.   Panel, 9 × 20 in.

By RUBENS.   Lent by SIR FRANCIS COOK, BART.

119. DEATH OF HIPPOLYTUS. A Sketch.

In the foreground the body of Hippolytus, who has fallen out of his chariot ; the affrighted horses are dashing against one another ; on the left are a sea monster and a triton.   Panel, 20 × 25 in.   Smith, *Cat. Rais.*, Vol. ii., p. 178.

By RUBENS.   Lent by the EARL BROWNLOW.

120. VENUS AND ADONIS.

In a wooded landscape at the foot of a large tree, Venus, reclining, is supported by Adonis ; on the left is Cupid with arrow and quiver, and on the right two dogs ; at the feet of Venus lies a horn and a quiver hangs on the tree.   Panel, 16½ × 28 in.

By RUBENS.   Lent by SIR WILLIAM FARRER.

121. THE TRIUMPHAL PROCESSION OF HENRI IV. AFTER THE BATTLE OF IVRY.   A Sketch.

The king is represented standing in a gorgeous car, embossed with ornaments in gold ; he holds an olive-branch in his hand, and is clad in splendid armour, with a grey mantle over his shoulders ; Victory attends him, and is placing a wreath on his uncovered head ; the four white horses which are attached to the car are led by females, and guided by Minerva ; numerous soldiers with banners, trophies, and instruments of music accompany the car, which is followed by a train of captives ; the victorious troops who lead the van are entering the gates of a city ; the victor is hailed by men and women with their children, some of whom are seated. Canvas, 18¾ × 32½ in.   A sketch for the large picture in the Florence Gallery.   See Smith, *Cat. Rais.*, vol. ii., p. 260.

By RUBENS.   Lent by the EARL OF DARNLEY.

122. THE FAMILY OF RUBENS.

A company of ladies and gentlemen, in which the painter has introduced portraits of himself, his family and others, assembled in a flower garden ; most of them are seated in the parterre near the entrance to a chateau, and are engaged in conversation and music : amorini hover around, in the branches overhead and on the edge of a fountain, on which is perched a peacock.   Panel, 49 × 67 in.

This picture is better known under the title of " The Garden of Love." There appears to be several versions of it, which differ somewhat in their composition. See Smith, *Cat. Rais.*, ii., pp. 86, 132 and 166.

By RUBENS.   Lent by the DUKE OF LEEDS.

123. THE FOUR EVANGELISTS.   A Sketch.

The four Evangelists, attended by their various attributes, are seen setting forth on the divine behest to preach the Gospel. Foremost are St. Matthew and St. Luke ; St. Mark follows, carrying an open book, to a page of which an angel, flying by his side, is pointing ; St. John follows behind ; architectural frame, with festoons of flowers and fruit and cherubim.   Panel, 25 × 26 in.

A sketch for the large picture in the possession of the Duke of Westminster. See Waagen, vol. iv. p. 109.

By RUBENS.   Lent by CHARLES MORRISON, ESQ

D

124.   St. Ildefonsus Receiving the Chasuble.   A Sketch.

Within a sacred edifice, the Virgin, seated, is giving the chasuble to St. Ildefonsus, who kneels before her and kisses the robe ; the Virgin is surrounded by four female saints ; in the wings kneel the Infanta Isabella and her husband, the Archduke Albert of Austria ; behind them stand their patron saints.   Panel, 16 × 25½ in.

A sketch for the splendid altarpiece formerly in a church near Brussels, now in Vienna. See Smith, *Cat. Rais.*, vol. ii., p. 91.

By RUBENS.   Lent by G. E. MARTIN, ESQ.

125.   Jan van Scorel, Painter (1495–1562).

So-called from his birthplace, Schoorl, near Alkmaar ; studied under various masters in his own country, of whom Mabuse was one ; afterwards visited Venice and Jerusalem, whence he returned by Rhodes to Rome ; made by Pope Adrian VI. Keeper of the Art Collections of the Vatican ; after the Pope's death he returned to his native country and settled at Utrecht, where he died.

Bust, facing, in brown fur-lined coat, black cap, small white ruff.   Panel (circular), 22¼ in.

By SIR ANTONIO MORE.   *1560*   Lent by the SOCIETY OF ANTIQUARIES.

126.   A Landscape.

In the foreground are peasants returning from the harvest ; beyond is seen a waggon, drawn by two horses, descending a hill ; on the right, a hill with windmills ; in the distance are a village and a chateau, the landscape stretching far back to the sea. Panel, 14 × 28 in.

This picture is etched in Young's "Grosvenor Gallery," where it is stated to have been painted by Rubens before he went to Italy, and when he was only eighteen or twenty years of age.   Smith, *Cat. Rais.*, ii., p. 250.

By RUBENS.   Lent by the late DUKE OF WESTMINSTER, K.G.

127.   The Conversion of St. Paul.   A Sketch.

Landscape ; in the foreground St. Paul thrown from his horse lies on the ground, and is supported by a soldier ; others, on horseback, and on foot, are in attitudes of alarm ; above, in the clouds, the figure of the Saviour.   Panel, 17 × 10¾ in.

By RUBENS.   Lent by the late DUKE OF WESTMINSTER, K.G.

128.   Portrait of the Artist's Brother, Philip.

Three-quarter length figure, seated to right, his right hand on his hip ; left resting on his knee ; black dress, white ruff and cuffs ; crimson curtain behind ; on right landscape.   Panel, 43 × 34 in.

By RUBENS.   Lent by SIR FRANCIS COOK, BART.

129. DIANA AND HER NYMPHS REPOSING AFTER THE CHASE.

Diana and two nymphs, naked, are reposing on a bank after the fatigues of the chase; the goddess reclines on her back against a tree, and one of the nymphs, from whom a satyr is drawing off a white covering, is recumbent at her side; the remaining nymph is more retired on the right; in the background are seen other satyrs, and in the foreground the spoils of the chase and a sleeping dog. Canvas, 84 × 121 in. Painted about 1616; it belonged to the Duke of Buckingham, at whose death it was probably bought by Charles I. See Smith, *Cat. Rais.*, vol. ii. p. 238.

By RUBENS and SNYDERS.   Lent by HER MAJESTY THE QUEEN (Hampton Court).

130. PORTRAIT OF A LADY (Sister [?] of the Painter's Wife).

Three-quarter-length figure, standing to left, looking towards the spectator; hands folded; black satin dress, pearl necklace and earrings, jewelled chain and pendant with pearl drop on her dress; curtain and sky background. Inscribed "Virgo Brabantina." Canvas, 42 × 31 in.

By RUBENS.   Lent by CHARLES BUTLER, ESQ.

131. ORPHEUS AND EURYDICE. A Sketch.

The scene represents a view of the infernal regions; Pluto grasping his trident and seated on his throne, with Proserpine habited in black by his side; the dog Cerberus lies at their feet; on the opposite side are Orpheus and Eurydice; the former, with his lyre, is retiring cautiously from the presence of the deities, followed by Eurydice, who is naked all but the loins, has long dark hair floating on her shoulders; the portal of the gloomy regions stands open before them, and beyond is seen the river Styx. Panel, 11 × 12½ in. Smith, *Cat. Rais.*, ii. p. 136.

By RUBENS.   Lent by MESSRS. P. AND D. COLNAGHI AND CO.

132. THE WAGGON. A Landscape.

View in a woody country, crossed by a stream; on the right going down a steep bank to the water is a waggon drawn by two horses, one of which is ridden by the driver; on the other side of the stream are clumps of trees; setting sun. Panel, 19¼ × 21¼ in. From the Reinagle, Mulgrave, Camden, and Rogers Collections. See *Catalogue of the Northbrook Collection*, No. 88. Smith, *Cat. Rais.*, vol. ix. p. 331.

By RUBENS.   Lent by the EARL OF NORTHBROOK, K.C.I.E.

133. THOMAS HOWARD, EARL OF ARUNDEL, K.G. (1586–1646).

Son of Philip, Earl of Arundel, married Aletheia, daughter of the seventh Earl of Shrewsbury; was the first collector of works of Art in England; the famous collection of inscriptions known as the Arundel marbles was brought to this country by him.

D 2

Half-length, life-size, figure to left ; hair and beard dark and bushy ; he is dressed in a fur-lined mantle and a plain falling collar ; the George, attached to a ribbon, is suspended in front. Canvas, 26½ by 21 in. Engraved by Houbraken. Smith, *Cat. Rais.*, ii. p. 308.

By RUBENS.   Lent by the EARL OF CARLISLE.

134. THE RAINBOW. A Landscape.

A landscape, exhibiting a mountainous country, divided in the centre by a winding river, crossed by a bridge, near which are several cottages ; a second bridge, formed of planks, crosses the river near the front ; in the foreground are a flock of sheep and several figures ; the latter consist of a shepherd seated at the foot of a tree on the left, who appears to have just ceased playing his pipe, and is looking earnestly at a beautiful rainbow, which crosses the heavens in the opposite side ; near him stands a peasant, directing the attention of a woman to a couple who are reclining on the ground together ; the appearance of a recent shower pervades the surrounding scene. Canvas, 45½ × 66½ in.
Similar pictures are at the Hermitage, St. Petersburg, and at the Louvre. Smith, *Cat. Rais.*, vol. i., p. 293, and vol. ii. p. 119.

By RUBENS.   Lent by LORD WINDSOR.

135. THE DAUGHTER OF HERODIAS RECEIVING THE HEAD OF ST. JOHN
THE BAPTIST.

Three-quarter length figures of the daughter of Herodias and an attendant, holding the charger on which the executioner has just placed the head of St. John. Canvas, 48 × 45 in. From the Orleans Collection. Smith, *Cat. Rais.*, vol. ix. p. 308.

By RUBENS.   Lent by the EARL OF CARLISLE.

136. PORTRAIT OF THE PAINTER.

Flemish painter of portraits and conversations ; born at Antwerp in 1614, studied under David Ryckaert, was official painter to the Count de Monterey, Governor-General of the Low Countries, and was employed by Charles I., the Archduke Leopold, and the Prince of Orange ; died in 1684.
Three-quarter length, life-size figure, front, head turned to right and looking upwards, long brown hair, black coat and cloak, white cuffs and collar ; his left hand is placed on his waist ; pillar to left. Canvas, 41¼ × 33½ in.

By GONZALES COQUES.   Lent by H. L. BISCHOFFSHEIM, ESQ.

137. A LANDSCAPE.

A landscape, with trees and rivulet on the left ; in the foreground a horse feeding ; moonlight scene. Panel, 25½ × 35 in. From the Dudley Collection.

By RUBENS.   Lent by LUDWIG MOND, ESQ.

138. PORTRAIT OF JOHN DE WITT (1625—1672).

Eminent Dutch statesman ; born at Dort, was pensionary of Holland ; in 1667 he succeeded in carrying an edict for the abolition of the office of Stadtholder, which proved his own ruin, when the Prince of Orange resumed the title in 1672 ; was barbarously murdered, with his brother, Cornelius, by the populace.

Small three-quarter length figure, seated towards right, looking at the spectator, in black cloak, lace collar ; right hand holding a scroll and resting on the back of a chair ; landscape background. Canvas, 22½ × 17½ in.

By GONZALES COQUES. Lent by G. E. MARTIN, ESQ.

139. FIGURES AND DEAD GAME.

A tall handsome woman, in red dress and blue petticoat, and carrying a basket of fruit before her, is approaching from the left side, accompanied by a sportsman, who with a hawk on his left hand, has thrust his arm under hers, and is helping himself to some figs from the basket ; three dogs accompany him ; one of them is by the side of the woman, the others are smelling the game, which, consisting of a wild boar, fawns, hares, pheasants, and other birds, lie in ample abundance on the left of the picture. Canvas, 80 × 88 in.

This picture, when in the collection of the Earl of Thanet, was engraved by R. Earlom, under the title of "The Fig." It subsequently belonged to the Earl of Plymouth. Smith, *Cat. Rais.* ii. p. 276.

By RUBENS. Lent by LORD WINDSOR.

140. PORTRAIT OF THE WIFE AND SON OF JOHN DE WITT. (See No. 138).

Small three-quarter length figure seated to left in a garden, in brown dress and black mantle, large falling lace-collar and white cap ; her left hand holds on her knees a basket, and her right is placed on some fruit on a ledge, behind which is her son, who offers her an apple with his left hand ; he is dressed in black coat, white falling collar, and black hat. Canvas, 22½ × 17½ in.

By GONZALES COQUES. Lent by G. E. MARTIN, ESQ.

141. ABRAHAM AND MELCHISEDEK.

A composition of twenty figures ; in the centre Abraham, bare-headed, clad in armour and crimson mantle, advances towards Melchisedek, who presents him with two loaves ; Melchisedek wears a crown of olive, and a crimson mantle held by a page ; behind him stands a man with a basket of bread on his back, and on his right are four persons, two of whom are distributing bread to some soldiers ; beyond there are other soldiers and a youth holding Abraham's horse ; in the immediate foreground are two men with pots of wine ; the subject is enclosed within an architectural frame with cherubs and drapery. Panel, 26¼ × 32¼ in.

From the Palazzo Nuovo, Julienne, Trevor, Nieuwenhuys, &c., and Barry Collections. See *Catalogue of the Northbrook Collection*, No. 87. "A finished study of superlative excellence for the large picture in the collection of the Earl of Grosvenor." Smith, *Cat. Rais.*, ii. p. 184.

By RUBENS. Lent by the EARL OF NORTHBROOK, K.C.I.E.

142. THE DISMISSAL OF HAGAR.

Scene before a house ; Abraham looks out from the door, whilst Sarah raising her right hand dismisses Hagar ; at their feet a dog. Panel, 29 × 41 in. From the Agar Collection. Smith, *Cat. Rais.*, ii. p. 173.

By RUBENS.   Lent by the late DUKE OF WESTMINSTER, K.G.

143. THE WILD BOAR HUNT.

In a woody landscape a party consisting of huntsmen on foot and horseback accompanied by dogs, attacking a boar near the trunk of a fallen tree ; several of the dogs have seized the animal, whose progress is opposed by men on foot armed with javelins and spears, and one with a horn ; on the right two other horsemen are galloping up to the attack, and on the left is a boy holding two dogs in a leash ; through an opening in the forest is seen another party in pursuit of wild boars. Canvas, 54 × 66 in.
From the Nevel, King of Holland and Adrian Hope Collections. The original sketch for this picture is in the Dresden Gallery. Smith, *Cat. Rais.*, ii., p. 276.

By RUBENS.   Lent by the CORPORATION OF THE CITY OF GLASGOW.

144. PORTRAIT OF A GENTLEMAN.

Half-length figure, slightly turned to right, head facing, in grey coat trimmed with silver braid, crimson cloak and white cravat, long brown wig. Canvas, oval, 28 × 23 in.

By SIR GODFREY KNELLER, BART.   Lent by WHITWORTH WALLIS, ESQ.

145. DANIEL IN THE DEN OF LIONS.

The prophet is represented seated on his red cloak, naked, in the middle of the den his hands clasped, and his countenance directed upwards with an expression of earnest prayer ; nine lions are prowling around him ; skull and bones in the foreground. Canvas, 87 × 129 in.
Rubens, writing of this picture from Antwerp, 18th April, 1618, said, " Daniel amidst many lions taken from the life – original, the whole by my hand." Engraved by Blooteling Van der Leuw and Lamb, and in mezzotint by J. Ward. Included in the Catalogue of Charles I., where it is stated that it was presented to that monarch by Lord Dorchester. Smith, *Cat. Rais.*, ii. p. 162. Waagen, iii., p. 294.

By RUBENS.   Lent by the TRUSTEES OF THE LATE DUKE OF HAMILTON.

DRAWINGS BY RUBENS.

LENT BY SIR CHARLES ROBINSON.

146. THE FOUR QUARTERS OF THE GLOBE. Drawing for the large picture at Vienna.

147. THE OUTSKIRTS OF A RUINED FLEMISH CHATEAU. Landscape in colours. Early period.

148. THE DEFEAT OF SENNACHERIB. Finished study for a portion of this composition. Chalk heightened with pen in bistre.

149. THE GARDEN OF LOVE. Finished drawing for the picture in the Madrid Gallery. Bistre heightened with white.

150. THE GARDEN OF LOVE. Another finished drawing for the picture in the Madrid Gallery. Bistre heightened with white.

151. A FEMALE SAINT ENTOMBED BY ANGELS. Black and red chalk washed with bistre. For a picture of the Master's early period.

152. PETER AND JOHN AT THE BEAUTIFUL GATE. After Raffaelle's Hampton Court Cartoon. Finished drawing in bistre heightened with white.

153. THE OUTSKIRTS OF A RUINED FLEMISH CHATEAU. Landscape in colours. Early period. Companion to No. 147.

154. THE TRIUMPH OF CÆSAR. After Giulio Romano ; Mantuan period. Highly finished drawing in bistre heightened with white.

155. THE INFANT SAVIOUR AND ST. JOHN WITH A LAMB. Black chalk. Rubens's early period.

156. STUDY OF A MAN IN A VOLUMINOUS CLOAK. Black chalk.

157. STUDY OF FEMALE FIGURES FOR AN ALLEGORICAL SUBJECT. chalk.

158. THE ADORATION OF THE MAGI. Finished pen drawing in bistre.

159. THE VISION OF EZEKIEL. After the picture by Raffaelle. Highly finished drawing in red chalk.

160. DIANA SURPRISED. Chalk drawing washed with India ink.

161. SENECA IN THE BATH. Finished pen drawing in bistre by Rubens for the engraving by Cornelius Galle.

162. SENECA IN THE BATH. Engraving from the above by Cornelius Galle.

163. STUDY FOR THE HEAD OF A HUNTSMAN BLOWING HIS HORN. For the picture of the "Wild Boar Hunt" in the Collection of Sir Charles Robinson (see Picture, No. 117).

164. THE ARCHDUKE ALBERT, GOVERNOR OF THE NETHERLANDS, ON HORSEBACK. Finished drawing in chalk and water-colours.

SOUTH ROOM.

PICTURES OF THE BRITISH SCHOOL.

170. PAPIRIUS PRAETEXTATUS AND HIS MOTHER.

Papirius Praetextatus, entreated by his mother to disclose the secrets of the Senate, tells her it had been debated whether it would be more useful to the Republic for the husbands to have two wives or the wives to have two husbands. The day following the Roman ladies went to the Senate House to request that the wives might have two husbands each to the great surprise of the senators. Praetextatus, being present, related the answers he had made his mother to avoid revealing the business of the State, which ingenious artifice was highly applauded.

The mother of Papirius Praetextatus in white, gold embroidered robe and gold sash, is seated in front of a large building, and is greeting her son, whose right hand she clasps and places her left under his chin ; he wears a pale blue toga and red cloak, and, raising his left hand, looks at his mother with a perplexed expression. Canvas (circular), 24½ in.

By ANGELICA KAUFFMAN, R.A.   Lent by COL. SIR EDMUND ANTROBUS, BART.

171. GENERAL JAMES WOLFE (1726-1759).

Celebrated general ; born at Westerham in Kent, entered the army at an early age ; distinguished himself at Dettingen, Fontenoy, Falkirk, Culloden and Minden ; commanded in Canada and was killed at Quebec, Sept. 13th, 1759.

Half-length figure, life-size towards left, head facing, in dark blue uniform with red facings, white powdered wig ; his right hand is thrust into his coat. Canvas, 29½ × 24½ in.

By THOMAS GAINSBOROUGH, R.A.   Lent by MESSRS. P. AND D. COLNAGHI AND CO.

172. PORTRAIT OF A LADY.

Three-quarter length figure, life-size, seated to left, in white dress and white headdress ; right arm resting on chair ; hands crossed ; long brown hair falling over right shoulder. Canvas, 28½ × 24 in.

By GEORGE ROMNEY.   Lent by LIONEL PHILLIPS, ESQ.

173. Elizabeth (Gunning) Duchess of Hamilton and Argyll (1734–1790).

Younger daughter of John Gunning, of Castlecote, and sister of Maria, Countess of Coventry, married first, James, sixth Duke of Hamilton, and secondly, John Campbell, Marquess of Lorne, afterwards fifth Duke of Argyll. She was noted for her beauty, and "even in advanced life and with very decayed health she was remarkably beautiful and seemed composed of a finer clay than the rest of her sex."

Full length, life-size figure, leaning on a sculptured pedestal ; white dress, and red mantle, lined with ermine ; landscape background with doves on the right and flowers on left. Canvas, 94 × 58 in.

Painted in January, 1759. Exhibited at the Society of Arts in 1760, and at the Grosvenor Gallery in 1884

By Sir Joshua Reynolds, P.R.A.

Lent by the Trustees of the late Duke of Hamilton.

174. Portrait of a Lady.

Half-length figure, to left, head looking at the spectator, white dress ; brown hair. Canvas, 21½ × 17½ in.

By John Hoppner, R.A.   Lent by Lionel Phillips, Esq.

175. Mrs. Earle.

Three-quarter length life-size figure seated to left, looking at the spectator, hands folded on her lap ; white dress and gold ribbon with pink rose at her waist ; landscape background. Canvas, 29 × 24½ in.

By Sir Thomas Lawrence, P.R.A.   Lent by Lionel Earle, Esq.

176. Lady Holte, Wife of Sir Charles Holte, of Aston Hall.

Half-length life-size figure to left, head turned to the spectator, hands crossed ; black dress, white fichu, and white cap. Canvas, 29 × 24½ in.

By George Romney.   Lent by the Corporation of the City of Birmingham.

177. A Landscape.

Hilly landscape ; in the foreground a piece of water and herdsmen taking cattle to drink ; two cottages on the right ; a road on the left. Canvas, 24¼ × 29½ in.

By John Constable, R.A.   Lent by Lionel Phillips, Esq.

178. Portrait of a Girl and a Dog.

Three quarter-length figure seated, facing, in a landscape, nestling a dog in her arms ; red and white dress ; brown hair with red ribbon. Canvas, 29¼ × 24½ in.

By Sir Joshua Reynolds, P.R.A.   Lent by Lionel Phillips, Esq.

179. A LANDSCAPE WITH LAKE NEMI.

View of the lake and the surrounding country ; in the foreground are two men, one seated on a log, and a woman ; and before them a man in a boat ; a ruined temple in the distance. Canvas, 17½ × 22 in.

By RICHARD WILSON, R.A.   Lent by SIR JAMES D. LINTON.

180. ELIZA FARREN, AFTERWARDS COUNTESS OF DERBY (1759-1829).

Actress ; daughter of a surgeon at Cork ; appeared at the Haymarket Theatre in 1777 ; married, as his second wife, Edward, twelfth Earl of Derby, 1797.
Sketch of head, looking to right ; hair long and powdered. Canvas (oval), 18½ × 15 in.

By SIR THOMAS LAWRENCE, P.R.A.   Lent by WENTWORTH BEAUMONT, ESQ.

181. THE MARKET CART.

A landscape ; in the foreground is a market cart, drawn by three horses. which are about to cross a rivulet, and the foremost of which is held by a youth ; in the cart are two women with their children and a boy and a man, who is assisting another woman to mount ; in the foreground are dogs and sheep. Canvas, 47¼ × 58 in.

By THOMAS GAINSBOROUGH, R.A.   Lent by LIONEL PHILLIPS, ESQ.

182. MADAME GIOVANNA BACELLI (d. 1801).

Celebrated dancer ; appeared in London in 1779, and was most popular for some years. Walpole writes of her as dancing at Paris in 1788 with a blue bandeau on her head, having on it the motto of the Garter. She died in Sackville Street, Piccadilly, 7 May, 1801, generally respected for her benevolence.
Small, full-length figure turned to the right, dancing ; she looks at the spectator, and holds a white scarf in both hands, the right being placed behind her back ; white dress and hat, trimmed with blue ribbons. Canvas, 21¾ × 15½ in.

By THOMAS GAINSBOROUGH, R.A.   Lent by ALFRED BEIT, ESQ.

183. HEAD OF A BOY. A Sketch.

Head of a boy in profile to right ; encircled by a band with a jewel in front. Canvas, 14½ × 13 in.

By SIR JOSHUA REYNOLDS, P.R.A.   Lent by SIR WILLIAM FARRER.

184. PORTRAIT OF MASTER HARE.

Three-quarter length figure of a child seated to left in a landscape, right hand pointing upwards ; white dress with lilac sash ; auburn hair. Canvas, 29 × 23½ in.

By SIR JOSHUA REYNOLDS, P.R.A.   Lent by LIONEL PHILLIPS, ESQ.

185. COAST SCENE. '

In the foreground three men, launching a boat ; three fishing smacks on the right. Canvas, 20 × 24 in.

By JOHN CONSTABLE, R.A.   Lent by LIONEL PHILLIPS, ESQ.

186. PORTRAIT OF A LADY.

Half-length figure, life-size, front, head turned to left, white dress, lilac shawl falling . over her arms ; powdered hair ; landscape background. Canvas, 29 × 23½ in.

By RICHARD COSWAY, R.A.   Lent by LIONEL PHILLIPS, ESQ.

187. SIR JOHN STANLEY, 1ST LORD STANLEY OF ALDERLEY (1766–1850).

Bust, life-size, to right, black coat, white collar and cravat, and wig. Canvas, 29½ × 24½ in.

By JOHN HOPPNER, R.A.   Lent by the HON. LYULPH STANLEY.

188. JANE MAXWELL, DUCHESS OF GORDON (d. 1812).

Daughter of Sir William Maxwell, married 8th October, 1767, Alexander, fourth Duke of Gordon.

Three-quarter length figure, seated, facing, in a landscape, holding a dog on her lap ; white dress and fichu ; her hair bound with a green ribbon. Canvas, 35½ × 26¾ in.

By GEORGE ROMNEY.   Lent by COL. SIR EDMUND ANTROBUS, BART.

189. WALTON BRIDGES.

View of the Thames, with Walton Bridges ; in the foreground are men with sheep, whilst others are placing some on boats. Canvas, 35 × 48 in. Painted for the Earl of Essex.

By J. M. W. TURNER, R.A.   Lent by JAMES ORROCK, ESQ.

190. MRS. NESBITT AS "CIRCE."

Mrs. Nesbitt was the mistress of Augustus John, third Earl of Bristol, who besides leaving her a large estate, bequeathed to her half his personal property, which was estimated at £30,000. This portrait, which is considered one of Reynolds's master-pieces as a subject portrait, was painted for Lord Bristol. It was presented by the Marquess of Bristol to Sir John Stanley.

Three-quarter length figure seated to left, in the character of Circe ; white dress; she holds in her right hand a wand ; at her side a panther and a white cat ; in the fore-ground a goblet on a table ; in the background trees with monkey. Canvas, 49 × 39 in.

By SIR JOSHUA REYNOLDS, P.R.A.   Lent by the HON. LYULPH STANLEY.

191. NEWARK ABBEY.

In the foreground is the River Wey, with a water-mill and barges and boat ; in one of the former is seen a man seated at a fire, and in the latter a man washing vegetables ; on the left trees ; distant view of the ruined Abbey. Canvas, 35 × 48 in. Painted for Lord de Tabley.

By J. M. W. TURNER, R.A.   Lent by JAMES ORROCK, ESQ.

192. LADY HAMILTON (1761[?]–1815).

Born in humble life ; noted for her beauty, and became a favourite model to Romney. She also sat to Reynolds, Hoppner and Lawrence. Married in 1791 Sir William Hamilton, and was the object of Lord Nelson's passionate attachment.
Three-quarter length figure seated to left, looking back over her left shoulder, her head resting on her left hand ; white dress and cap, and coloured sash. Canvas, 29 × 24½ in.

By GEORGE ROMNEY.   Lent by COL. SIR EDMUND ANTROBUS, BART.

193. THE RIGHT HON. EDMUND BURKE, M.P. (1729–1797).

Statesman, orator and writer ; born in Dublin, entered Parliament in 1765 as member for Wendover, elected for Bristol in 1774, and for Malton in 1787 ; he specially distinguished himself by his speeches on the American question, on Catholic Emancipation and in the prosecution of Warren Hastings. Died at Beaconsfield, July 8, 1797.
Half-length figure, life-size, front, head turned to left ; in crimson cloak with fur collar, brown waistcoat and white stock. Canvas, 30 × 24¼ in.

By SIR JOSHUA REYNOLDS, P.R.A.   Lent by COL. SIR EDMUND ANTROBUS, BART.

194. CHARLES LENNOX, FOURTH DUKE OF RICHMOND (1764–1819).

Son of Lord George Henry Lennox, succeeded to the dukedom in 1806 ; was Lord Lieutenant of Ireland, 1807–1812 ; appointed Governor of Canada in 1818, and died there in 1819.
Half-length life-size figure to left, head looking at the spectator, in military dress, Star of the Bath. Canvas, 30 × 24½ in.

By JOHN HOPPNER, R.A.   Lent by MESSRS. P. AND D. COLNAGHI AND CO.

195. ANNE LUTTRELL, DUCHESS OF CUMBERLAND (d. 1803).

Elder daughter of Simon Luttrell, afterwards Earl of Carhampton ; married first Christopher Horton, of Calton House, Derbyshire, and secondly Henry Frederick, Duke of Cumberland, brother of George III.
Life-size to the waist, turned towards left, and looking to right ; arms crossed ; pink low-cut dress, white fichu trimmed with pearls ; gauze scarf ; blue ribbon in her hair. Canvas, 36 × 28 in.

By THOMAS GAINSBOROUGH, R.A.   Lent by LORD WENLOCK.

196. MARIA WALPOLE, COUNTESS WALDEGRAVE, AND DUCHESS OF GLOUCESTER (1737–1807).

Daughter of Sir Edward Walpole, K.B.; married, first, James, second Earl Waldegrave; and, secondly, William Henry, Duke of Gloucester, son of Frederick, Prince of Wales, by whom she was the mother of William Frederick, second Duke of Gloucester, and Princesses Sophia and Caroline.

Three-quarter length figure to right, looking at the spectator; her right hand holds her train on her hip; white gold embroidered dress; on her head feathers and jewels; from her head depends a long veil, which passes over her left shoulder; landscape background.   Canvas, 50 × 40 in.

By THOMAS GAINSBOROUGH, R.A.   Lent by ALFRED BEIT, ESQ.

197. A LANDSCAPE.

On the left is a cottage, in front of which stand two boys leaning on a paling, one of whom points to a man with a gun in the distance and two dogs; before the cottage is another man, who holds a white horse by the bridle; sea in the distance.   Canvas, 27¼ × 35½ in.

By GEORGE MORLAND.   Lent by LIONEL PHILLIPS, ESQ.

198. FRANCESCO BARTOLOZZI, R.A. (1725–1815).

Celebrated engraver; born at Florence, came to England in 1764; was appointed engraver to the King, and in 1768 was made a Royal Academician.   In 1802, Bartolozzi accepted the post of Director of the National Academy of Lisbon, where he died in 1815.

Half-length life-size figure facing, head turned to left; his arms resting on a table on which are some papers; crimson velvet coat, trimmed with fur, pale grey waistcoat and white stock.   Canvas, 29¾ × 24½ in.

By SIR JOSHUA REYNOLDS, P.R.A.   Lent by the Earl of MORLEY.

199. THE REV. JOHN H. GRAY AS A YOUTH AGED 13.

Three-quarter length figure standing towards left, looking at the spectator, his right hand resting on a stick, his left on his hip; blue coat, grey waistcoat and trousers, large white collar; landscape background.   Canvas, 50 × 40 in.

By SIR HENRY RAEBURN, P.R.S.A., R.A.
          Lent by MAJOR CHARLES ANSTRUTHER-THOMSON.

200. MRS. REBECCA MINET (1743–1819).

Wife of Daniel Minet (see No. 201) and daughter of —— Sturt (or Stert), lived after her husband's death at Richmond, Surrey, where she died, 18 April, 1819.   Her name has been added to her husband's in Bengeo (old) church.

Half-length, life-size figure, to left, in low-cut pink dress trimmed with strings of pearls; hair powdered, and entwined with pearls; earrings of pearls.   Canvas (oval), 29 × 22½ in.

By THOMAS GAINSBOROUGH, R.A.   Lent by H. L. BISCHOFFSHEIM, ESQ.

201. DANIEL MINET, F.R.S., F.S.A. (1729–1790).

Son of Daniel Minet and Anne Maria Atkyns ; was admitted to the Inner Temple, (1759) ; Surveyor of H.M's Customs ; Fellow of the Royal Society (1767) and of the Society of Antiquaries (1767) ; lived in Grosvenor Street and More Park, Herts ; and was buried at Bengeo. In the old church there is a tablet to his memory bearing his arms. He was grandson of Isaac Minet, a Huguenot refugee from Calais, who settled at Dover.

Half-length life-size figure front, head looking to right ; brick-red coat and waistcoat, lace ruff and stock, white wig ; hat under left arm. Canvas (oval), $28\frac{1}{4} \times 23\frac{1}{4}$ in.

By THOMAS GAINSBOROUGH, R.A.   Lent by WILLIAM MINET, ESQ.

202. CHILD WITH A DOG.

Child kneeling, facing, her arms around the neck of a dog ; white frock ; landscape background. Canvas, $29\frac{1}{2} \times 24\frac{1}{2}$ in.

By JOHN HOPPNER, R.A.   Lent by CHARLES BUTLER, ESQ.

203. MRS. DE BERGH.

Half-length figure, seated, to left, and looking at the spectator ; her right arm rests on a ledge ; her right hand holds her green girdle ; white dress ; pearls in her hair ; foliage background with blue sky. Canvas, $29\frac{1}{2} \times 24\frac{1}{4}$ in.

By GEORGE ROMNEY.   Lent by GEORGE DONALDSON, ESQ.

204. MISS LARPENT.

Full length life-size figure of a girl seated on a bank in a landscape ; she holds in her arms a rabbit ; white dress over pink skirt, black cape lined with pink, white cap and red shoes. Canvas, 50×40 in.

By GEORGE ROMNEY.   Lent by the MISSES DE HOCHEPIED LARPENT.

CASE A.

IN WEST ROOM.

COLLECTION OF WORKS OF ART LENT BY SIR CHARLES ROBINSON.

207. DRINKING HORN, mounted in silver gilt, with a statuette of St. Michael. Spanish or French work, second half of the fourteenth century. Obtained from the Church del Carmen at Carrion de los Condes, Spain.

208. STATUETTE OF THE VIRGIN AND CHILD, silver gilt. French work, *circa* 1350. Obtained from the Convent of Castejon de Monegros, betwixt Huesca and Teruel, Spain.

209. ST. CHRISTOPHER, statuette in metal gilt repoussé work, the face, hands, and feet in silver. Spanish, second half of the fourteenth century.

210. INCENSE BURNER, bronze, damascened withgold and silver. Saracenic work, thirteenth century.

211. INKSTAND IN SILVER AND TRANSLUCENT ENAMEL. Hispano-Moresco work, probably made at Granada, end of the fifteenth century.

212. ROSEWATER SALVER, silver gilt repoussé work in high relief embossed with figure subjects of Spanish Knights fighting with Moorish Emirs. Spanish or Portuguese work, *circa* 1490.

213. STANDING CENSER, silver repoussé work. Spanish, *circa* 1480.

214. CASKET, silver repoussé work. Italian, *circa* 1500–1520.

215. IVORY CASKET, with lock and handles in gold, set with cabochon sapphires. Portuguese-Indian work, made at Goa, to contain chrismal phials, *circa* 1530.

216. PYX, FOR THE RESERVATION OF THE BLESSED SACRAMENT, ivory mounted, in metal gilt. North of France work, *circa* 1250.

217. SWORD "ESTOQUE," the hilt in copper, originally gilded, and inlaid with silver. Italian, end of the fifteenth century.

218. SWORD ANELACE OR COURTE EPÉE." French, *circa* 1450.

219. DAGGER, the hilt in steel, gilded and gold inlaid, the grip ivory stained green. Italian, probably Milanese work, *circa* 1530.

220. DAGGER "MISERICORDE," the hilt in steel, originally gilt and silvered, and enriched with translucent enamels, the blade inscribed, "Salus per Christum." Spanish work, *circa* 1280—1300.

221. DAGGER "MISERICORDE," with steel hilt, originally gilded, *circa* 1350—1400.

222. NAUTILUS SHELL CUP, mounted in silver gilt. Spanish work, *circa* 1500—1520.

CASE B.

IN WEST ROOM.

COLLECTION OF WORKS OF ART LENT BY SIR CHARLES ROBINSON.

223. MONSTRANCE RELIQUARY, metal gilt, with crystal receptacle. Italian *circa* 1450. From the Church of Santa Maria Maddalena at Perugia.

224. RELIQUARY CROSS, in silver gilt and gold, enriched with translucent enamel and jewels. Made by order of Robert of Anjou, King of Hungary, *circa* 1346, to contain a relic of the true cross.

E

225. PRAYER DESK, in bronze gilt and steel. Spanish work, *circa* 1520. Believed to be the work of the celebrated Spanish master, Becerril, of Cuenca. Obtained from the owners of a private chapel in the Cathedral of Valencia.

226. MANUSCRIPT BOOK, bound in velvet, with silver gilt mounting. The book is the statutes of a guild or corporation at Toledo, *circa* 1560.

227. BRONZE GROUP, HERCULES AND CACUS, by Giovanni de Bologna. A reduction by the artist from the colossal marble group executed for the Cardinal Duke of Lerma.

228. ROSEWATER EWER AND PLATEAU, silver gilt, repoussé work. Spanish *circa* 1500—1520, recently obtained from an ancient family in Toledo.

229. CANDLESTICK, bronze inlaid with champlevé enamel. Rhenish-Byzantine work, *circa* 1150.

230. ITALIAN BRONZE DOOR-KNOCKER, *circa* 1560.

231. LUCRETIA KILLING HERSELF, alto-relievo in lead, originally painted. Italian work, middle of the fifteenth century, ascribed to Donatello.

232. SILVER SALVER WITH REPOUSSÉ ORNAMENTATION. Spanish-American work, probably made at Lima, first half of the seventeenth century.

233. INCENSE BURNER IN THE FORM OF A LION STANDING ON A PLATEAU. Silver repoussé work, richly chased. Spanish-Colonial work, probably made at Lima. First half of seventeenth century.

234. ARCHAIC GREEK BRONZE STATUETTE OF A DRAPED FEMALE FIGURE.

235. ANTIQUE GREEK BRONZE STATUETTE. A Winged Victory.

236. ANTIQUE GREEK BRONZE STATUETTE. Venus.

237. ANTIQUE GREEK BRONZE STATUETTE. A Faun.

238. ANTIQUE GREEK BRONZE STATUETTE. Minerva. Found at Aquileia, the Ancient Venice.

239. ANTIQUE GREEK BRONZE STATUETTE. A Girl.

240. SEVENTY-FIVE CAMEOS, selected from a collection of antique Greek and Roman gems. Card No. 1 contains seven cameos from the Marlborough and Barberini collections, including (A) the celebrated cameo engraved in the illustrated last century work on the Marlborough gems, and (B) the Barberini Medusa.

CENTRAL HALL.

CASE C.

EMBROIDERY.

241. AN ITALIAN EMBROIDERED COPE.   End of the fifteenth century.
Lent by SIR CHARLES ROBINSON.

CASE D.

242. ORPHREYS FOR A CLOTH OF ESTATE OR HANGINGS OF A THRONE.
The arms and devices indicate it to have been that of the
Emperor Maximilian and his wife, Mary of Burgundy.   End of
the fifteenth century.
Lent by SIR CHARLES ROBINSON.

CASE E.

243. VARIOUS EMBROIDERED ORPHREYS OF THE FOURTEENTH AND
FIFTEENTH CENTURIES.
Lent by SIR CHARLES ROBINSON.

BALCONY.

FLEMISH SCHOOL.

244. THE CRUCIFIXION AND THE CONVERSION OF ST. LONGINUS.

Longinus, the centurion, who pierced the side of the Saviour, seeing the wonders and omens which accompanied His death, exclaimed, "Truly this Man was the Son of God." Shortly after he had uttered these words he placed his hands stained with the blood of our Lord, before his eyes, and immediately a great imperfection and weakness in his sight, which had afflicted him for many years, were healed ; and he turned away repentant and was shortly afterwards baptised. Jameson, *Sacred and Legendary Art*, vol. ii., p. 788.

In the centre is Christ crucified ; on the left are the four Marys : and behind them the centurion, St. Longinus, on horseback, raising his hands towards his face ; his spear, with which he has pierced the Christ, is held by an attendant ; on the right are two horsemen with attendants, and in the background a view of Jerusalem. Panel, 41 × 33 in.

EARLY FLEMISH SCHOOL.   Lent by SIR HENRY H. HOWORTH, K.C.I.E, M.P.

245. ST. LAURENCE SHOWING THE TREASURES OF THE CHURCH.

The prefect of Rome having been informed that St. Laurence had under his care the treasures of the Church, consisting of money and gold and silver vessels, and had hidden them away, commanded him to reveal where the treasures were concealed. St. Laurence declined to reveal his charge, but three days afterwards gathered together the sick and the poor to whom he had dispensed alms, and placing them before the prefect, said, "Behold, here are the treasures of Christ's Church."

St. Laurence, standing at the entrance of a building, is showing to the prefect and others the "treasures of Christ's Church" in the form of the poor and maimed of the city ; in the background are houses. Canvas, 51¼ × 35¾ in.

Said to be a wing of the lost altarpiece at Alkmaar.

EARLY FLEMISH SCHOOL.   Lent by SIR HENRY H. HOWORTH, K.C.I.E., M.P.

246. SCENES FROM THE LIFE OF ST. MARY MAGDALENE. THE SAINT IN PALESTINE.

This picture and No. 247 depict various scenes in the life of St. Mary Magdalene The legend is, that Mary Magdalene, having inherited vast riches and possessions from her father, Syrus, abandoned herself to luxurious pleasures ; but Martha, her sister, who was a model of virtue and propriety, rebuked her for her wanton habits, and at length persuaded her to listen to the exhortations of Jesus, through which her heart was touched and converted. After the ascension of Christ, Lazarus, with his sisters, Martha and Mary and others, was set adrift in a vessel without sails, oars or rudder : but guided by Providence they were safely landed in a harbour which proved to be Marseilles. Here the people were pagans : but after a while they listened to the eloquent preaching of Mary Magdalene and were converted and baptised. Among the many miracles attributed to the Magdalene there is one which became popular in art. A Prince of Provence arriving at Marseilles with his wife, and being desirous of having a son, invoked the intercession of Mary Magdalene, by whose persuasive eloquence he had been partly converted to Christianity. Mary promised that his desire would be granted if he would be wholly converted and baptized. Shortly afterwards on his journeying to Jerusalem with his wife a son was born to the prince ; but the mother dying he landed on a rocky island and placing the dead body in a cave, left the infant son beside her, after committing it to the care of the Saint. On his return journey he touched at the island to weep over his wife's grave. Now, wonderful to relate, the infant child had been preserved alive by the prayers of the Magdalene, and was accustomed to run on the sands of the seashore to gather shells and pebbles. When the child perceived the strangers he ran to hide himself under the cloak which covered his dead mother, and the father and all who were with him were filled with astonishment ; but their surprise was still greater when the woman opened her eyes and stretched out her arms to her husband. Having offered up thanks they all returned to Marseilles and received baptism from the hands of Mary Magdalene. From that time all the people of Marseilles became Christians. See Jameson, *Sacred and Legendary Art*, Vol. i., pp. 346 and 376.

A cavalcade proceeding to the chase ; the figures are habited in costumes of the period of the painting of the picture ; in the foreground Mary Magdalene seated on a white horse with a falcon on her left wrist, wears a rich brown embroidered robe lined with ermine, and red hat ; in the background she is seen with her sister Martha listening to Christ preaching ; behind are two disciples and three others ; in the distance a castle. Panel, 47½ × 29¼ in. From the Ruston Collection.

Attributed to QUINTEN MATSYS.   Lent by MESSRS. P. AND D. COLNAGHI AND CO.

247. SCENES FROM THE LIFE OF ST. MARY MAGDALENE. THE SAINT IN PROVENCE. (See No. 246.)

In the foreground Mary Magdalene, habited as in No. 246, but with white mantle and head-dress, standing facing between two trees, her left hand resting on a cross-bar, and preaching to assembled pagans ; in the background is depicted the miracle of the mother and the child, a ship on the sea at the mouth of a harbour approaches the shore, on which runs a naked child ; the dead mother lies within a cave ; on the right a kneeling monk looking up at a vision. Panel, 47½ × 29¼ in. From the Ruston Collection.

Attributed to QUINTEN MATSYS.   Lent by MESSRS. P. AND D. COLNAGHI AND CO.

248. THE DEPOSITION.

The dead body of the Saviour lying on the ground, supported in the arms of St. John ; the Virgin with clasped hands kneels beside Him, and three other holy women behind ; Joseph of Arimathea and another stand by ; landscape background, with representations of the *Ascension* and the *Resurrection*. Panel, 41 × 20 in. From the Roscoe Collection. Waagen, iii., p. 235.

By MICHAEL WOHLGEMUTH.

Lent by the TRUSTEES OF THE ROYAL INSTITUTION, LIVERPOOL.

249. A LANDSCAPE.

' View of a wooded landscape, with many houses and city, and sea in the distance ; in the centre of the picture is a wide road, along which are passing men and women on foot, on mules and on horses. Panel, 26½ × 41¾ in.

By HERRI DE BLES (CIVETTA). Lent by the TRUSTEES OF THE BOWES MUSEUM.

250. VIEW FROM RICHMOND HILL.

On the right a terrace, amidst trees, commanding an expansive view of the valley of the Thames. Canvas, 52 + 48¼ in.

By RICHARD WILSON, R.A. Lent by COL. SIR EDMUND ANTROBUS, BART.

PHOTOGRAVURES

251. THE VISITATION.

By JOACHIM PATINIR. In the National Gallery.

Lent by THE CATHOLIC ART SOCIETY.

252. THE FLIGHT INTO EGYPT.

By JOACHIM PATINIR. In the National Gallery.

Lent by THE CATHOLIC ART SOCIETY.

LENT BY THE BERLIN PHOTOGRAPHIC SOCIETY.

253. PHILIP LORD WHARTON.

By VAN DYCK. In the Hermitage, St. Petersburg.

254. ISABELLA BRANDT.

By VAN DYCK. In the Hermitage, St. Petersburg.

255. SIR THOMAS CHALONER.

By VAN DYCK.   In the Hermitage, St. Petersburg.

256. GEORGIANA DUCHESS OF DEVONSHIRE AND HER CHILD. An artist's proof engraving on Japanese paper.

By REYNOLDS.   In the Chatsworth Collection.

257. SIR A. VAN DYCK : AS A YOUTH.

By VAN DYCK.   In the Hermitage, St. Petersburg.

258. SUSANNA FOURMENT AND DAUGHTER CATHERINE.

By VAN DYCK.   In the Hermitage, St. Petersburg.

259. WILLIAM PRINCE OF ORANGE.

By VAN DYCK.   In the Hermitage, St. Petersburg.

260. HENRIETTA MARIA

By VAN DYCK.   In the Dresden Gallery.

261. FAMILY GROUP.

By VAN DYCK.   In the Hermitage, St. Petersburg.

262. THE CHILDREN OF CHARLES I.

By VAN DYCK.   In the Dresden Gallery.

263. HELEN FOURMENT.

By RUBENS.   In the Hermitage, St. Petersburg.

264. THE CHILDREN OF CHARLES I.

By VAN DYCK.   In the Dresden Gallery.

265. LAZARUS MAHARKIJUS.

By VAN DYCK.   In the Hermitage, St. Petersburg.

266. VENUS AND ADONIS.

By RUBENS.   In the Hermitage. St. Petersburg.

267. CHARLES I.

By VAN DYCK.   In the Dresden Gallery.

INDEX OF PAINTERS.

Bles, Herri de, called Civetta (c. 1480-1551), 13, 49, 249
Bouts, Dierick (d. 1475), 42, 62, 78

Campana, Pedro (1503-1570?), 4
Cleef, Justus van (c. 1520-1556), 93
Cologne, Early School of, 1
Constable, John, R.A. (1776-1837), 177, 185
Coques, Gonzales (1618-1684), 104, 136, 138, 140
Cornelissen, Jacob (c. 1475-1553), 26, 40
Cosway, Richard, R.A. (1740-1821), 186

David, Gheeraert (c. 1483-1523), 10, 32, 52
David, Gheeraert, School of, 85
Death of the Virgin, Master of the, 43, 75
Dyck, Anthony van (1599-1641), 103

Eyck, Hubert van (c. 1366-1426), 27
Eyck, Jan van (c. 1380-1440), 9, 20, 27, 69, 82
Eyck, Jan van, School of, 38

Flemalle, Maitre de, 48
Flemish School, Early, 7, 15, 16, 22, 23, 24, 25, 30, 34, 44, 45, 47, 50, 53, 56, 57, 63, 64, 66, 68, 72, 77, 88, 89, 95, 98, 244, 245

Gainsborough, Thomas, R.A. (1727-1788), 171, 181, 182, 195, 196, 200, 201
Goes, Hugo van der (c. 1405-1482), 17, 33, 41, 51, 65
Gossaert, Jan, called Mabuse (1470?-1541), 3, 6, 8, 12, 29, 31, 36, 61, 70, 71, 84, 97

Hemessen, Jan Sanders van (painted 1519-1548), 55
Hoppner, John, R.A. (1758-1810), 174, 187, 194, 202

Kauffman, Angelica, R.A. (1741-1807), 170
Kneller, Sir Godfrey, Bart. (1646-1723), 144

Lawrence, Sir Thomas, P.R.A. (1769-1830), 175, 180

Leyden, Lucas van (c. 1494-1533), 79, 83, 86, 91
Lyons, Cornelius de (dates not known), 46
Mabuse, see Gossaert, Jan.
Master, The, of the Death of the Virgin, 43, 75
Matsys, Quinten (c. 1466-1531), 90, 94, 96, 246, 247
Memlinc, Hans (c. 1430-1492), 21, 35, 39, 54, 58
More, Sir Antonio (1512-1582?) 37, 125
Morland, George (1763-1804), 197
Mostert, Jan (c. 1474-1555), 67, 74, 80, 92

Orley, Bernard van (c. 1491-1542), 5, 60, 76, 87

Patinir, Joachim, (c. 1490-1524), 14, 73, 81

Raeburn, Sir Henry, R.A., P.R.S.A. (1756-1823), 199
Reynolds, Sir Joshua, P.R.A. (1723-1792), 173, 178, 183, 184, 190, 193, 198
Romney, George (1734-1812), 172, 176, 188, 192, 203, 204
Rubens, Sir Peter Paul (1577-1640), 105, 107, 108, 109, 110, 111, 112, 113, 114, 115, 116, 117, 118, 119, 120, 121, 122, 123, 124, 126, 127, 128, 129, 130, 131, 132, 133, 134, 135, 137, 139, 141, 142, 143, 145
Rubens, Sir Peter Paul (1577-1640), Drawings by, 146-164

Scorel, Jan van (1495-1562), 28
Snyders, Franz (1579-1657), 129

Turner, J. M. W., R.A. (1775-1851), 189, 191

Vinckeboons, David (1578-1629), 18

Weyden, Rogier van der (c. 1400-1464), 2, 11, 59, 99
Wilson, Richard, R.A. (1740-1782), 179, 250
Wohlgemuth, Michael (1434-1519), 19, 248

INDEX OF EXHIBITORS.

Her Majesty the Queen, 84, 129

Antiquaries, Society of, 33, 125
Antrobus, Col. Sir Edmund, Bart., 170, 188, 192, 193, 250

Beaumont, Wentworth, Esq., 180
Beit, Alfred, Esq., 182, 196
Berlin Photographic Company, 253-257
Birmingham, Corporation of, 176
Bischoffsheim, H. L., Esq., 136, 200
Bodley, G. F., Esq., A.R.A., 21
Bowes Museum, Trustees of, 93, 249
Brocklebank, Ralph, Esq., 83, 87, 89, 90
Brownlow, Earl, 97, 110, 119,
Butler, Charles, Esq., 35, 37, 38, 49, 74, 80, 130, 202

Carlisle, Earl of, 133, 135
Catholic Art Society, 251, 252
Clarke, Mrs. Stephenson, 42, 54, 65
Colnaghi, Martin, Esq., 73
Colnaghi and Co., Messrs. P. and D., 92, 131, 171, 194, 246, 247
Cook, Sir Francis, Bart, 3, 4, 5, 6, 7, 8, 9, 10, 11, 12, 13, 108, 109, 118, 128
Cook, Frederick L., Esq., M.P., 43
Crawford, Earl of, K.T., 85.
Crews, Charles, T. D., Esq., 23, 40, 78

Darnley, Earl of, 121
Donaldson, George, Esq., 203

Earle, Lionel, Esq., 175

Falcke, Isaac, Esq., 70
Farrer, Sir William, 86, 105, 120, 183
Flower, Wickham, Esq., 30, 44, 47, 57, 94

Gibbs, Antony, Esq., 17
Glasgow, Corporation of, 51, 143

Hamilton, Trustees of the late Duke of, 145, 173
Hardman, John, Esq., 22
Holford, Captain G. L., C.I.E., 29, 75
Howorth, Sir Henry H., K.C.I.E., M.P., 24, 28, 244, 245
Hughes, Hugh R., Esq., 96

Johnstone, George, Esq., M.D., 106

Lane, Hugh P., Esq., 18, 95, 104
Larpent, The Misses de Hochepied, 204
Leeds, Duke of, 122
Linton, Sir James, 179
Liverpool, Royal Institution of, 19, 41, 76, 77, 91, 248
Loreto Convent, The, Manchester, 25

Mackenzie, Sir Kenneth Muir, K.C.B., 81, 88
Martin, G. E., Esq., 103, 124, 138, 140
Minet, William, Esq., 201
Mond, Ludwig, Esq., 137
Morley, Earl of, 198
Morrison, Charles, Esq., 107, 123
Moulton, J. Fletcher, Esq., Q.C., M.P., 79, 82, 99

Northbrook, Earl of, 2, 55, 60, 61, 62, 63, 64, 66, 67, 68, 69, 71, 72, 132, 141

Orrock, James, Esq., 189, 191

Phillips, Lionel, Esq., 172, 174, 177, 178, 181, 184, 185, 186, 197

Robinson, Sir J. Charles, 1, 45, 117, 146-164, 207-243

Salting, George, Esq., 34, 46, 59
Smith-Barry, Rt. Hon. A.H., 111, 112, 113, 114, 115, 116
Somzée, M. Léon de, 15, 16, 20, 26, 27, 32, 48, 52
Stanley, Hon. Lyulph, 187, 190
Stowe, Alfred, Esq., 14
Sutton-Nelthorpe, R.C., Esq., 31

Thompson, Sir Henry, Bart., 58
Thomson, Major Anstruther, 199
Trevelyan, Lady, 50, 53, 56

Waller, J. G., Esq., 36
Wallis, Whitworth, Esq., 144
Wenlock, Lord, 195
Westminster, The late Duke of, K.G., 39, 126, 127, 142
Windsor, Lord, 134, 139

www.ingramcontent.com/pod-product-compliance
Lightning Source LLC
Chambersburg PA
CBHW021525270326
41930CB00008B/1104